Running Against the Tide

Running Against the Tide

the

True Tales from the Stud of the Sea

~~~~~~~~~~

CAPTAIN LEE ROSBACH

with Michael Shohl

G

Gallery Books

New York London Toronto Sydney New Delhi

Gallery Books
An Imprint of Simon & Schuster, Inc.
1230 Avenue of the Americas
New York, NY 10020

First Gallery Books hardcover edition September 2018

GALLERY BOOKS and colophon are registered trademarks of Simon & Schuster, Inc.

For information about special discounts for bulk purchases, please contact Simon & Schuster Special Sales at 1-866-506-1949 or business@simonandschuster.com.

The Simon & Schuster Speakers Bureau can bring authors to your live event. For more information or to book an event, contact the Simon & Schuster Speakers Bureau at 1-866-248-3049 or visit our website at www.simonspeakers.com.

Manufactured in the United States of America

10 9 8 7 6 5 4 3 2 1

Library of Congress Cataloging-in-Publication Data

Names: Rosbach, Lee, Captain, author. | Shohl, Michael, author.
Title: Running against the tide : true tales from the stud of the sea / by Captain Lee Rosbach ; with Michael Shohl.
Description: New York : Gallery Books, 2018.
Identifiers: LCCN 2018018266 | ISBN 9781501184444 (hardback)
Subjects: LCSH: Rosbach, Lee, Captain. | Television personalities—United States—Biography. | Ship captains—United States—Biography. | BISAC: BIOGRAPHY & AUTOBIOGRAPHY / Personal Memoirs.
Classification: LCC PN1992.4.R575 A3 2018 | DDC 791.4502/8092 [B]—dc23
LC record available at https://lccn.loc.gov/2018018266

ISBN 978-1-5011-8444-4
ISBN 978-1-5011-8446-8 (ebook)

*To my lovely bride, Mary Anne, who has been
through it all and put up with all of it through the years.
It's been a long and crazy ride, she just made it easier
and a lot more worthwhile.*

Running Against the Tide

Chapter 1

~~~~~~~~~

When the Horse Is Dead, Stop Kicking It

I didn't know why the bottom rung of the ladder worried me. The bottom one was the easy one. It was the one on the top that was going to kill me.

"Another day, another dollar," I said to myself, planting my foot on that bottom rung. It had no give in it, comforting since it was taking my weight and 40 pounds of welding gear. I swung my lifeline around a steel cable running up the length of the ladder, clipping in and moving up. The clamp was designed to allow movement upward but arrest any movement downward. A good policy to have. Only 400 feet to go to the top of the water tower.

I was working for Chicago Bridge & Iron, an outfit that built all kinds of enormous structures. For some jobs, it was smokestacks. For others, it was nuclear-containment vessels. Other times it was water towers. The one thing in common—it was all high steel, giant fabrications that required working in the sky between 400 and 1,000 feet up. Not many people worked that high, and I'd been more than a bit scared the first time I saw how far you could drop, but that was just motivation for me. Since I was a kid, I always wanted to go places other guys were afraid to go, do things others couldn't or wouldn't do. The fear let me know that it was worth my time, let me know the task passed my test. Now it was up to me, and I sure as hell wasn't going to quit. Nothing was going to kick my ass. I loved forcing myself out of my comfort zone.

The money wasn't too bad, either.

Working as a welder was a good job in 1975. They paid me $9 an hour to climb those ladders and fuse one piece of metal to another. That was enough in earnings in one day for a week's worth of groceries for me, my wife, and our five kids. I'd have a month's rent in just a few days of work. Not too shabby for a twenty-five-year-old with a growing family. The dangers didn't even seem like dangers when you're twenty-five. Mortality is something that happens to the other guy. The thing was, sometimes, you worked side-by-side with the other guy. And so did he. Hell, I was 10 feet tall, invisible and bulletproof—just ask me. That was the only time in my life that I knew everything. Been learning ever since.

Accidents happened. They happened with all too much regularity. Hell, in our southeast division, there were 600 boilermakers and laborers, and we'd lose 1 percent of those guys every year to accidents. Six men every single year. Breaking safety lines. Equipment failure. Acts of God. Lots of things can happen to a man at 800 feet in the air when he's holding a welding rod that burns at over 3,000 degrees, and not a lot of them good. A one-inch air arc used for melting steel can reach minimum temps of 6,500 degrees Fahrenheit. One time, a foreman hired his son, only eighteen, to work the site. He was on the ground, not even up in the scaffolding, when someone working above somehow lost his grip on a grinder. The machine weighed about 20 pounds, and from where it fell, it took about six seconds to reach the ground. Every second, it just got faster and faster. By the time it hit the kid, that 20-pound grinder was moving at about 130 miles per hour, and it took him out instantly. The ambulance came, took the body away. His dad never came back to the site. The rest of us? We waited for over an hour before the accident was squared away, then we got back to work. It sounds cold, but there was nothing else but work, and that was exactly what we needed at that point in time. Stay occupied.

I kept climbing up the ladder. I didn't want to think about the bad things that could happen, I just wanted to think about my safety and my job, what I needed to do. You overthink it, you can lose it. I'd seen that happen, too. Guys who were just like me, guys with more experience than me, who would go up every day to the job and then, one day—BOOM—it would just hit them like a flash of light: the danger, the risk. They'd grab on to the scaffolding with white knuckles, grip so tight you'd have to pry their fingers off with a crowbar. They couldn't climb down. The foreman would have to call 911 so they could come up with a basket and lower them down to the ground. One bad day could be the last day they'd ever spend on the high steel. The ability to focus was paramount.

Guys who've never done the work don't quite understand it. They might think that climbing a ladder fifty stories is just like climbing a ladder to fix their gutters, just a bit higher up. But it's not that way. When you're climbing something that big, going that high, you look up, and the ladder doesn't just look like it goes up, it feels like it's angling backward as you climb. So, you focus on the next rung and try not to think about the ladder bending backward, or then you may white knuckle the next grip, and they'd have to send a basket to get your dumb ass down.

I finally reached the top. It was so high up, I could literally see some very low-lying clouds below me, could see birds flying beneath me. When I first started the work, it took me six months before I was able to feel comfortable moving around. The first ninety days, anything that didn't move, I tied off to it. I was taking no chances. Of course, it slowed me down considerably, but I didn't care; I wanted to feel safe. Now I felt more secure. I walked to my spot, calm but aware. My workstation was waiting—a ladder hanging out over the rest of the world, anchored in by another one of the crew. These guys were professionals, like me, and they knew what they were doing. Still, it was my life hanging on the end of that ladder and dangling over a 400-foot drop. I gave the welding perch a good once-over. Trust but verify.

I pulled at my collar a little bit to get some more air. I was wearing what basically all the guys wore, a kind of informal welder's uniform: denim pants, T-shirt under a long-sleeve denim shirt, leather boots, and a leather cape sleeve covering my torso and back, leather sleeves down to the wrists, and welding gloves that went to the elbow. It was a lot of gear to be wearing in Biloxi, Mississippi, in June, but it helped keep you separated from molten metal that might come flying off the structure. We all wore our denim shirts untucked, not because we were slobs, but because you sure as hell didn't want any red-hot metal getting between your waist and your belt. Same reason why none of us wore lace-up work boots. You wanted to avoid molten slag getting caught in your laces and burning a hole through the top of your foot. If for some reason, God forbid, something got in that boot, we could slip it off without having to cut it off. That's the sort of thing that could ruin your whole day, not to mention the fact you would never walk again without a limp.

You'd think guys might wear steel-toed boots for the work, something tough that could take a pounding, but no one did. If you had something heavy fall on your foot, and such things weren't uncommon, you didn't want a plate of steel over your toes. If you're wearing just a good leather work boot when a 200-pound piece of metal falls on it, some of those toes are going to break. But if you're wearing steel-toed boots, the metal's going to pinch those toes right off. Better a broken toe than a severed one.

After all that climbing and hauling gear to your workstation, that's when the fun really began: the welding. The welding we did was all stick welding. I started the first pass with a welding rod for mild steel (6010) that held two pieces of metal together. Then I finished that with a low-hydrogen rod called 7018, the final interior weld on that seam. I welded uphill, starting at the bottom of the seam and moving upward to the top.

I made each pass until the thickness of the seam was overfilled so another crew, the QA (quality assurance) guys, could grind the weld down flat and X-ray it for flaws. Then I went on the outside of the structure and used a tool called an air arc, cutting out the first pass of 6010 that I'd put in and then welding up the outside of the seam. As soon as I finished the seam, techs came by to prep it for X-ray to see if there were any flaws in the welds. If there were, I'd have to go back in, cut them out, and redo them. On big structures that held a lot of weight and nuclear-containment vessels, they were all 100 percent X-ray work.

We got a bonus of 25 cents for every good foot of weld we put down, but for every bad picture they took they'd penalize us 50 cents and make us stop working, go back, and fix the fuckup. Hey, in the real world, you fuck up, there are consequences. So, if you weren't laying down new welds, you were losing money. It was called the picture bonus, so on top of the $9 per hour, I could make almost an additional $9 an hour by laying down good welds and not screwing up. If you didn't do your job well, theoretically, you could end up in the hole, which would lead to your immediate dismissal. The foreman always walked around with a pocket full of cash to pay off slackers and send them down the road. We used to call it two weeks and a road map. Now, that's incentive. Nobody wanted to lose their job and give up that good money. Hell, when you get paid that well, that's about a steak dinner for two with all the trimmings and a couple of drinks—every two hours—in a restaurant that a blue-collar guy like me had no business being in. Didn't mean I wouldn't enjoy it, but my edges were a bit rough.

Speed was important. That's why I carried my rod bag with another 25 to 30 pounds of welding rod. A can of welding rods weighed about 50 pounds, and I'd carry as much as I could. I wouldn't waste time going to the toolshed to get more or waiting on ground crew to send up more rods. Welding rods would have to be stored in a rod oven to keep all moisture out of the equation. The humidity would cause you to lay down bad welds and cost you money. All rods exposed longer than a couple of hours had to be put back in the oven to dry out.

Any way I could think of to save time, I'd do it. My lunch "hour" was the five minutes I'd need to shovel down the sandwich and apple I had in my lunchbox. There were no port-a-potties 50 stories up, so while some guys would climb down that ladder to hit the head, other guys would just relieve themselves off the side of the tower. It might sound uncouth, but the time saved could buy a man a nice new pair of boots. Taking a piss was expensive on the high steel. I'd even seen guys take a dump in an empty rod can and then heave it over the side. Worked great, except that one time the wind caught it and ended up spraying everyone's cars with shit from on high. Brought a literal meaning to the term "shit storm."

It may sound gross, but time was money. If we finished up the job before schedule and under budget, the crew got to split 40 percent of what we saved. If someone wasn't cutting it, he was messing with our money, and that would not be tolerated. This could be a problem with new guys. They didn't know the pace, didn't necessarily know how we did things, and they could slow us down. On our crew you did your job and did it right or we would make you pay, and it wasn't going to be pleasant. One time, and only once, a guy was such a damn slacker that the crew waited until he went to the port-a-potties and wrapped a welding rod through the hasp of the lock. Then they had the crane operator lift it up and shake it around before setting it down. We unlocked it, and the newbie came stumbling out, covered in shit and with a brand-new perspective. But a guy would have to really be dragging ass to get a code red like that.

It was thirsty work. I always worked in the southeast, in Alabama and Mississippi and Georgia and Florida, because I liked being able to work year-round and not have to worry about bad weather. But that also meant that I was wearing three layers of clothing, including a layer of leather, in Mississippi on a 100-degree day while blasting a steel plate with up to 6,500 degrees of heat. The company always provided salt pills to the crew so we'd retain water. And they'd send up these 10-gallon Igloo coolers full of water and ice so we didn't pass out. Just doing your job, it was easy to lose 7 pounds a day just from sweating. It sure made a man thirsty. For some, maybe even thirsty for something stronger than water.

And that's what nearly killed me.

When you're building something enormous, like a water tower, you have the crane you're using pull itself up to the next level. The crane climbs up the structure as you complete the lower portions. You're basically using the crane to disassemble and reassemble itself at a higher point on the structure. We call this "jumping the rig." We'd finished a lower level and were prepping the jump the rig. We worked it primarily as a three-man job. Two guys would sit on the base of the cage that housed the boom of the crane in wing seats and get raised to the next level, using steel pry bars to push the cage away from the welded seams, so it wouldn't get hung up. A crane operator sat 50 to 75 yards away, responding to our hand signals to go faster, slower, brake, or whatever we indicated. Crane signals on high steel are all uniform, so it's not something that you just make up as you go along.

I took one wing seat, and my brother-in-law, Scotty, took the other one. Scotty had been the one to help get me the job on the site.

"Watch that seam," he said, pushing out his pry bar.

That's when the world started to fall away.

The cage just started sliding down the cable that had been pulling us up. It wasn't a freefall, but we were going down, and picking up speed.

My right hand went to the straps holding me in place, as did Scotty's. We only had two options: We could stay on and hope that the cage offered some protection or cushion once we hit bottom. Or we could try to peel out and jump, maybe grab a cable on the way down.

Either way, the odds were good we were going to die.

We dropped about 50 feet in the three seconds before the brakes re-engaged. Longest three seconds of my life. It wasn't a sharp shock, not the immediate snap of a hangman's noose. The brake was designed to arrest a fall more gradually, so it wouldn't tear the equipment apart. And thank God it was, or the impact might have broken our backs.

Scotty and I caught our breaths.

"You okay?" he asked.

"Yeah. You?" I replied.

"Still alive," he said.

In most places, you fall five stories, the boss would say, "Take the rest of the day." Not us. We unstrapped ourselves and finished jumping the rig before heading down to solid ground.

It had only been about forty-five minutes, but that was plenty of time for Scotty and me to get pissed. You start with the adrenaline of almost dying, and then you add the realization that someone was responsible for what happened. Then that adrenaline is transformed from "survival" to "payback."

"You guys okay?" one of the other guys, Bill, asked.

"Getting there," I said.

"Shit, when I saw Clarence Irishing up his coffee this morning, I figured he was just feeling cold," Bill said. It was only a ten-man crew. If one guy heard or saw something, we'd all know it eventually.

"Yeah, Biloxi in summer can practically give you fucking frostbite," I said.

Goddamn Clarence. He was the crane operator. Classic Southern good ol' boy. Not much between the ears. He'd put whiskey in his coffee, and he must have let his foot slip off the crane's brake. And almost killed us.

Scotty started running his hand over his 5-pound sledgehammer like he was warming it up. We'd use the tool to beat down bull pins that we used for fitting, but I think Scotty now had another beat down in mind.

As soon as we got to the deck, Scotty had one thing on his mind. He slid that sledge out of his tool belt and made a beeline for Clarence. The crane operator was an older guy, maybe forty-five or so, and if Scotty had his way, he wasn't going to get one minute older.

Before Scotty could cave his skull in, he got wrapped up by our foreman, Carl Dover. Scotty was no stick figure. He was about 6'1", 195 pounds of solid muscle, chiseled by years of working high steel, but Carl had about 2 inches and 30 pounds on him. Carl was one tough son of a bitch, definitely the kind of guy you'd want on your side in a fight. The edges are pretty rough on boilermakers. Redneck boilermakers make New York City construction workers look like crossing guards. No offense to the trades in New

York, but these guys were something you had to see to believe. We never worked by local union laws. We were part of the international union and rules were different, if they existed at all. These guys would fight at the drop of a hard hat. Hell, sometimes they would even throw the hat to get things going.

"Easy, Scotty," Carl said. Scotty was no shrinking violet, but he wasn't so lost in his adrenaline rage that he wanted to mix it up with Carl.

"Clarence is out of here. I gave him his walking papers," Carl said. It was enough to get Scotty to holster his sledge.

It got my heart rate up, that's for sure. I was pretty shaken up. So shaken up that I took half an hour to let the tremors go away before going back up top to work. You can't make good welds while you're shaking, but you can't earn any bonus money if you're sitting one out. That's just how it worked. There's an accident, there's an injury, you treat it, you fix the equipment, and you get back to work.

And it's not like this put the fear of God into the rest of the crew. It was like playing a football game. A guy gets a concussion, tears an ACL, or dislocates a shoulder—that's rough, it's unfortunate, but that's his problem. Should have moved a little faster, should have practiced more, should have seen it coming. It's not a problem that's going to get solved by the rest of the team quitting.

I put everything in my bag at the end of the day—my lunchbox, my welder's helmet, my unused sticks. It was 40 to 50 pounds going up, and the same minus some water or coffee coming down. Carrying 50 pounds of gear down 400 feet of ladder after a full day of welding, and almost getting killed, can really tire a man. Some people wanted a faster way down.

Faster, on a 400-foot water tower, isn't always safer.

"You want the express, Lee?" said Frankie, another welder.

"Not today," I said.

"Suit yourself," he said, slipping on his welding gloves. He grabbed a 1½-inch steel cable hanging from the center post of the tower, smiled, and jumped off.

Jesus Christ, that was insane. The guy was basically falling 400 feet, just using his gloves to brake a little bit on the way down. And that's dangerous enough on a good day. His lifeline was just over an inch-thick braided steel wire. If he picked the wrong cable, one with a quarter-inch burr sticking out of it, that welding glove wouldn't stop it. The glove was good enough protection from the friction of holding the cable, but if he hit a steel stinger 100 feet down, it would tear right through that glove, rip out his flesh and tendons on the way. If he didn't bleed out, he'd sure as hell lose his grip and fall the rest of the way. But I never saw anyone fall using the express line.

Sometimes, I suppose, you just have to take a risk.

Eventually, I decided I wanted something more stable. I liked the work, liked the pay, but we'd always be moving. We'd complete a new job, we'd move on. You'd hope to work on a nuclear-containment vessel, because those would be two-year commitments. Otherwise, it was finish the project and move to another city. It was a good way to get exposed to different restaurants, but not a great way to get to know the neighbors.

I took a new job, working for Allis-Chalmers as a fabricator and then as a supervisor in the maintenance department of Midwest Steel outside of Gary, Indiana. The highest I ever worked there was maybe 80 feet off the ground, so it didn't have quite the adrenaline rush of the old days. I worked steadily for about five years before the work started drying up due to too much competition from overseas. I saw the writing on the wall and started moonlighting as a bartender to make a little extra money. When they closed the plant at Midwest, I was working nights and parties at the bar at the local chapter of the Elks Club.

It was there that I heard about another opportunity: running my own place. There was a bar that was available that I might be able to lease. The good news was that it was affordable. The bad news was that there were some good reasons it was.

One reason was that it was almost literally a shithole. The place stank and needed a power wash over every corner. The owner, Quinlan, was blind, but I guess he must have lost his sense of smell, too, because that place needed some serious work. We couldn't afford to hire it out, so I did it myself. We closed the place down for a month while I got it to where it needed to be. We cleaned, replaced carpet, built a DJ booth, a dance floor, everything we thought that we needed to make it work. We called the place, for no real reason other than it sounded like a proper name for a bar, J.D.'s Place.

Another reason that it was cheap was that the place was a biker bar. The local motorcycle club, the Devil's Diciples (they intentionally misspelled the word *disciples* so as not to give the impression they were part of any organized religion, as if that were likely), liked to use it as an unofficial clubhouse. So, it was loud and the regulars, the lifeblood of any bar, liked to get in fights every night and smash the place up. A slow night was only two fights. But hell, I liked a challenge. And I liked the idea of being my own boss.

You hear a lot of things about bikers, how the Hells Angels will gut you with a motor oil opener or how the Mongols all carry .44 Magnums or how the Gypsy Jokers eat the flesh of their enemies. Pretty lurid, cinematic tales of violence and debauchery. And maybe those guys really ride like that and fight like that and leave a trail of bodies in their wake. But these guys? I called them the Klingons. Not because they, or I, were huge *Star Trek* fans, but because they seemed to just attach themselves to things, like my bar. Not that they weren't dangerous, make no mistake about that. But I think they also wanted to pledge to be brought in to a larger organization, wanted to be an affiliate for a bigger club. That is to say, I didn't find them too intimidating. Though in hindsight, maybe I should have.

Maybe I just wasn't smart enough to be afraid, but I wasn't going to back down from these pricks. I sure as hell wasn't going to let them walk over me or let them tell me who ran *my* place. They had no respect for someone who just caved. You either stood up, or you got eaten alive. You've got to stand your ground, or you better just throw in the towel. I have a lot of four-letter words in my vocabulary, but "quit" doesn't happen to be one of them.

I let them know that they were welcome to come to my place to drink and have a good time, but they had to behave, in a manner of speaking. Their money was as good as anyone's. But I made it clear that I wouldn't tolerate them insulting or abusing women, random fighting, or basically any of the things they enjoyed doing. I wouldn't accept them trying to impress or intimidate the decent customers by showing off their knives or guns, which I would do my best to relieve them of at the door. Break my rules, and I'd show them the door, either peacefully or they could pretend it was Burger King, and they could have it their way.

It took more than a few busted heads to send the message, but that message finally started coming through, loud and clear. If someone tried to slap his girlfriend around in my place, he was going out the door. He had two options: conscious or unconscious. The first time it happened, I wasn't nervous. It wasn't my first fight.

Some guys like to get in fights because they want to talk a lot of smack. They bellow about how tough they are, and they hope that their friends hold them back. After a few insults, they feel big and nobody had to get hurt. But I wasn't squaring off with these guys so I could feel tough. I didn't get in someone's face just to talk shit. If I had to fight, my goal was to be the one walking away, not the one getting carried out.

"You're done here. Out," I told the biker.

"Ah, I don't think so," he said.

"You can walk out, or you can be carried out. Your choice."

If he threw a punch, I was ready. If he wanted to jaw some more, then he'd made the decision to get carried out. I had no problems decking a guy who couldn't listen.

There were lots of fights I had to break up, lots of guys I had to show the door. Eventually, they started to self-police. It was still a pretty boisterous crowd. We had live music every now and then, but mostly we used our DJ booth, which I manned nightly as it afforded me an elevated view of the whole bar and dance floor area so I could respond quickly if needed.

That's how I got a pretty nasty injury. A guy got out of line, and so I threw a punch, but it just didn't land right. I felt the pain in my wrist when I connected, but sometimes it hurts to hit people, so I didn't think much of it. Three days later, it was just getting more and more sore. I went to the doctor's and got the bad news: the wrist was broken. Then the worse news: it was torn up pretty bad. Over the next two and a half years, I'd get four surgeries, two bone grafts, and ligament repair before I was finally "healed." Still, I'd rather endure the pain and grief than to acquiesce to people who are trying to take my livelihood away. I am and always have been a proud man. I take care of my own. My ability to feed and take care of my family was paramount to me. Do the right thing, or I would make you pay, even if it cost me personally.

Eventually, we got the place to where we wanted it to be. We upgraded to playing videos for entertainment, some Eagles and Phil Collins and the *Miami Vice* theme. People stopped coming in looking for a fight as a way to pass the time. When I was working the bar, I could start looking for empty glasses to fill instead of constantly looking for hands slipping under leather jackets, reaching for concealed weapons. Things were getting better.

That turned out to be a mistake, of sorts. While Quinlan, the owner, may have been blind (I never knew how he lost his sight), he could still see a good thing when it was in front of him. I'd made the bar respectable, made it safe, and that meant I'd also turned it into a moneymaker. Quinlan was one of those rare people who liked money, and he responded in kind. When it came time to renew our lease, he told me that business seemed so good, I shouldn't mind paying triple what we'd originally agreed to if I wanted to continue. I told him thanks but no thanks. J.D.'s Place would just have to find a new location.

That's, in part, how I found out about paradise.

It's a cliché that people talk to the bartender, but some clichés exist because they're rooted in reality. My trip to paradise came about because someone wanted to talk to the guy pouring the drinks.

A friend of mine, Kelly, had been visiting Grand Cayman in the Caribbean, and on the way back had stopped off in Provo (Providenciales) in Turks and Caicos.

"You ever been to Turks and Caicos, Lee?" he asked.

"Hell, I've never even seen the ocean," I replied.

"This place is amazing. You can see the ocean from pretty much any point on the land. And if you like running a restaurant and bar here in Indiana, wouldn't it be even better to run the same kind of place in a tropical paradise?"

"I don't know. We have the Pacers, after all. Then again, that might not actually be a selling point."

"It's like out of a dream."

Maybe it was the kind of dream worth visiting.

Carl Hiaasen, the crime novelist, once talked about how criminals made it easier for him to be a writer because they did so many flamboyant, crazy things in Florida. When asked why Florida and not Detroit, he said, basically, "If you had a choice, would you rather be a car thief in Detroit or Miami?" There's going to be people everywhere, but you're going to get a more colorful group where the sun shines and the drinks have umbrellas in them.

Not everyone dreams of living on a tropical island. My wife, Mary Anne, took a little convincing. She thought it was kind of a harebrained scheme.

"What do we know about living in another country?"

"They speak English there. It would be like moving to Florida."

"How many times have you even been on a plane?"

"Just once or twice. That means that this time, it would still be fun and exciting. Not old hat, like for jet-setters."

"Do you even own a passport?"

"Don't need one. I checked. Just a driver's license and a birth certificate."

"That's all we need?"

"That's it."

"Then what could possibly go wrong?"

We weren't crazy. We didn't just fly in, throw money on the bar, and become islanders. But I was intrigued, so I flew out to Turks and Caicos to check it out. After I landed in Provo, there's a place they take you called Oohh-Aahh Hill, because that was the sound you made when you got a load of the view. Just incredible. The place that was up for lease had a great view and was located not merely on the water, but literally built *over* the water. I just had to get it. It would mean breaking the lease on the current J.D.'s Place, which I'd never done before, but I just wasn't going to be denied.

When I returned from my recon, I'd proved to Mary Anne that I'd been able to successfully cross the water. Other than that, she was pretty right-on-the-money about me being out of my depth.

We became islanders.

Well, not exactly. We weren't natives to Turks and Caicos, and that turned out to be a pretty significant detail. We could run the restaurant, but we couldn't own it outright. We leased it from the owner, along with our apartment. And since I wasn't a native, I had to get a work permit, which was a pretty significant ding at $2,000 per year. It seemed wrong that I'd have to pay the cost of a car in order to have the pleasure of working twelve hours a day, but that's how it was done.

You'd think living on a tropical island would be easy. You do your job, you make money, and if you don't, you just eat coconuts and mangoes that fall from the trees and sleep on the beach. But hell, if it were that easy, that's what everybody would be doing.

And that's not what everybody was doing.

Running a business as a foreigner in an unfamiliar country presented quite a few challenges. For instance: water was expensive. You'd be surrounded by it, but if you wanted your ice cubes to taste refreshing instead of salty, you'd have to buy water, and it wasn't cheap. Electricity was more expensive than rent, mostly as a way to power the refrigeration. We had to pay $800 per month for the rent, and $1,400 per month just for the electric.

In short order, I started to realize we were seriously underfinanced. When I decided to lease the new place, I didn't realize that milk in Provo sold for $8 per gallon, which was about what it would cost for two tickets to the movies. There were only two grocery stores, and in short order, I figured out that they seemed to have an understanding to keep their prices as high as possible. There was no price war between those two operations. So, if we had any hope of staying in business, we'd have to import things from the States, and that plane only landed once a week.

It wasn't just like going to a new place when we moved to Provo—it was like moving to a new time period, in a past where technology was still a bit lagging. While computers in 1980 weren't as ubiquitous as they are now, banks could still move money around fairly quickly. But in Provo it was like going to a banana republic from the fifties. Everything was done by hand on ink-stained ledgers. If you wanted to get a check cashed, you'd have to spend hours waiting for people to review all the accounts by hand, checking ledgers and calling other banks. It would take forever to complete the simplest transaction.

That wasn't confined to the banking industry. Turks and Caicos was an island paradise, and they seemed to take their laid-back casual pace surprisingly seriously. Part of the business of a bar owner and restaurateur like myself was getting meat, fruit, vegetables, and all manner of perishables delivered. But getting it to the island wasn't the same thing as getting it to our restaurant.

I arrived at the customs office. "I'm here to pick up fifty pounds of ground beef and fifty pounds of frozen chicken," I told the first guy I saw. I assumed he'd take me to the tarmac so I could quickly inspect the shipment and take it to my place. Not so.

"Get in line," the customs official said.

I looked at the line. There were already twenty people waiting.

"There isn't somebody here who just does perishables?" I asked. "Or is there a refrigerated storage unit you use?"

"You have to stand in line. First come, first served."

That seemed fair but also maddening. So, I waited. I had no choice. I could even see through a window in the back of the customs office where my shipment was resting on the tarmac. Just sitting there in the hot sun, getting less and less frozen, and more and more worthless.

Finally, with just one person left in front of me, the customs agent running the line for receiving said, "It's lunch time. Please come back in two hours."

Wait—what? They closed the customs office for lunch? That seemed absurd. And they took *two hours* for lunch, every day? I told the man that I needed my food before it spoiled.

"You're in luck."

"Oh yeah?" I asked.

"You're second in line."

"But what do I do now? The office is closed for lunch."

"You can come back in two hours. But usually, the line starts forming very quickly. People want to conduct their business."

"I can only imagine."

"Or you can wait here, where you're second in line."

"You want me to wait here for two hours doing nothing? I've already been here for two hours waiting to get this far."

"It's up to you."

It's a special kind of torture watching perfectly good food spoil on hot pavement over the course of four hours because no one at the customs office knew what the hell they were doing. I suppose if they had a clue, they'd be working at the local supermarket charging me $8 a gallon for milk.

So, there was incompetence. But at least that was rooted in indifference. The bigger problem was the corruption.

It wasn't like the island was some kind of Mecca for organized crime, but there was the law, and then there was how things were done. And those two categories didn't always have a ton of overlap.

If you wanted to hire someone for your business, they had to be a native of Turks and Caicos, or I could pay another $2,000 in work permits. We were doing a lot of work in our restaurant, which meant that we had to hire a guy to work the bar, another couple of guys to work as waiters. In short order, we learned that the bartender, Fred, was stealing.

I was working in the kitchen when I came out to see how the front of the house was faring.

"How's it going out here?" I asked Fred.

"It's okay," he said.

I took a look at his tip jar—it was practically overflowing. We must be doing a little bit better than "okay."

"How's the till? Plenty of change?" I asked.

He ejected the cash drawer. Bare bones. There was more money in the tip jar than the register, which was never a good sign.

"You helping yourself to the till?" I asked. "Getting an advance?"

"It's no problem," Fred said.

"Hell, yes, it's a problem. That's my money in that tip jar."

"No, you don't understand. This is how it works."

"Not at my place."

I gave him his walking papers. I thought that, by firing a guy stealing from me, I'd be saving money. But because I fired a native, I then had to pay him three months' severance. It's the kind of thing that really promotes employee retention, even if they are ripping you off.

Turned out that skimming was just how business was done down there. Like a tip. They even had a word for it: "teefin'." For the pleasure of paying him to serve drinks, I could expect him to pocket about a buck for every drink he poured.

So, Fred was out, and we replaced him with Timothy. Timothy seemed like a great guy to have on the team. He was tall, handsome, really outgoing, and smart. He'd gone to college in the States, so I figured he'd be an improvement over Fred. But Timothy wasn't above teefing, either. Just the cost of doing business in the islands.

Still, I assumed that I could weather that storm. Part of what brought me to the island was that they were going to be opening a hotel and casino in Provo. Casinos meant gamblers, which meant lots of tourists coming into town to eat, drink, and be merry. Unfortunately, the casino investors ran out of money a year after we arrived, with only two floors of the property built, so not only did it mean that I couldn't count on the business from the customers, but I couldn't even count on the business from the construction workers I was expecting to build the place.

We were already cash-poor when we arrived, and those setbacks made us cash-starving. We had no choice but to close up our place on the waterfront and get a smaller, cheaper place instead. I found a spot in a strip mall that seemed ideal. It wasn't the dream location we had before, but it would serve as a decent breakfast and lunch spot until we could build our bankroll a bit.

Again, the law required that, as a non-native, I needed a partner, so we asked Timothy to be our business partner. He could help us get permits, hire staff, all the things we'd need. The good news was that he had a lot of energy.

The bad news was that some of that energy came from smoking crack.

Drugs were a huge problem on the island back then, and Timothy got pulled into it. And while we had hoped his college degree would be a great asset to us as a business partner, there's nothing worse than an educated thief.

"Lee—I'm going to need another five hundred for some work permits for the restaurant."

"Kind of steep, isn't it?" I asked.

"Is there anything on this island that isn't more expensive than it should be?"

"True enough," I said, getting him the money.

Cash came in, and then got quickly converted to crack. He blew through all our money. Our little breakfast and lunch place never even opened its doors. Maybe we could have hung on a little longer, but when the horse is dead, stop kicking it.

We were down to our last $75 when I saw an ad in a dive shop, a posting for a sailboat captain looking for a mate. No experience required. If there was one thing I had in abundance, it was no experience. I signed up.

I'd never even seen the ocean until I came to Turks and Caicos. And now I was being paid to sail through it.

It was a basic sailing ship, a basic delivery. There were four guys on, working in four-hour shifts. We'd sail to St. Martin, then they'd provide me my ticket back to Provo, plus $50 a day for the time at sea. It seemed like a fortune.

"Can you take orders?" the owner asked.

"You pay in cash?" I answered.

"Cash once we've come in to port."

"Then I'll do whatever you say."

We were both pretty desperate. A match made in heaven.

That's when I discovered I was a bit vulnerable to seasickness. I did my job, then went to my bunk to wretch. I didn't eat for six days. But damn, I loved it from the moment I got on board. Walking off the dock in St. Martin, the captain handed me a huge wad of cash. It seemed like all the money in the world.

It was only after I'd boarded the plane home that I realized I was only given half the money I'd been promised. It may seem rude to count the cash you're handed, but business is business.

Trust but verify.

I told Mary Anne when I got home that a career change was on order and that this was what I wanted to do.

Chapter 2

If You're Going to Be Dumb, You'd Better Be Tough

"I hear you need a job?"

The question sounded simple and straightforward enough, even charitable. But the key word was "need," and when someone knows you need something, they're not planning on giving you charity. It's not the kind of offer that ends with a fat salary and plush benefits. It's the kind of offer one might hear if someone wanted a getaway driver for a stickup.

And I did need the job.

I was living in Turks and Caicos, where I'd come with my wife to be the owner and operator of a bar and restaurant. But the restaurant wasn't doing good business. I'd worked as a deckhand as a way to make some extra money, and now I knew I wanted to work on boats. I wanted the wide-open water and the smell of salt air and the feel of the undulating, living sea under my feet. But if I wanted a captain's license, I needed time on the water. I needed days at sea.

To get my Coast Guard Captain's License, I'd need 720 days of boating experience, which meant 720 days underway and offshore. So, if I spent every day I could at sea, I'd have my license . . . in, hopefully, under five years.

I needed the days.

"What's the job?" I asked.

"It's a crossing. Two-man job, you and me. Some guy needs us to take his sailboat to the British Virgin Islands. We'll head out, fuel up in the Dominican Republic, top off in Puerto Rico, then drop it off in BVI and we fly home. Should just be a few days. No more than a week."

As a guy who liked precision, something about this plan bothered me. Measure twice, cut once, that kind of thing. And setting out on a sail to the British Virgin Islands, I wanted a better sense of the time. There's a big difference between two days and seven days. But hell, maybe it was a win-win. Either I finished early, or I'd get more days for my license. And I needed the days.

"How much does it pay?" I asked.

"A sweet two hundred and fifty dollars."

So somewhere between $35 and $125 a day, depending on how long we were gone. If I was able to book those kinds of jobs every day, I'd pull in about $27,000 for the year. These kinds of jobs weren't going to make me rich. But I wasn't doing it for the money.

I just needed the days.

"Sure, George," I said, extending my hand. "Let's do it."

"Great," he said, shaking mine. "Come to the pier on Monday morning around sunup and we'll head out." Then he was walking away, out of my restaurant and down the street. Lots to do before Monday.

It seemed like a simple job. But, as is often the case, "simple" doesn't always mean "easy."

George Larson was a character. The island was full of characters. Lots of runners came to the island. There are two types of runners: people running away from something or people running to something. Jimmy Buffett said it best. "Some of them are running from lovers, leaving no forward address, some of them are running tons of ganja, some are running from the IRS. You find it all in a banana republic." My wife and I came here, running to the lure of adventure, of opening a restaurant, the promise of warm weather, easy fishing, and having a business of our own in the islands. George, I figured, was running from something, I just wasn't sure what. I did know people on the island called him Crazy George, so that had to count for something.

Maybe that should have given me more doubt, should have served as a warning that I shouldn't be getting on a sailboat with a guy named Crazy George. But there are lots of reasons a guy gets called crazy. Maybe he just liked to party. Or maybe he was unconventional, like a lot of sailors can be. Or maybe he did things differently than the average captain. Or maybe he was just out of his mind.

I would later learn that, for Crazy George, it was all of the above.

For the most part, what earned him his nickname was that he operated solo. He'd take jobs delivering boats single-handed, just George at the helm for days on end. He was still alive, so he must have some skills, I figured.

Still, not all good sailors make good captains.

George had been in my restaurant before, hadn't caused any trouble, and he had a reputation on the island as a competent sailor. He certainly looked like what one might expect a sailor to look like. He was covered in tattoos, days-old stubble on his face, and projected the air of a pirate. Sandy blond hair from too much sun, deep tan from the same. He wasn't a joiner or a follower. He lived life on his own terms.

Crazy George.

My new captain.

"Permission to come aboard," I said to George, who was stowing some gear on the sailboat, the *Morgan*.

"What? Yeah, like I give a fuck," he said, waving at me lazily. Not big on ceremony was George.

The *Morgan* was a pretty small vessel, about 26 feet from stem to stern. It was a single-hull boat, with a bench in front of the steering wheel in the cockpit area, then a couple of steps down to an enclosed cabin with a galley equipped with a small two-burner stove working off a liquid fuel, no generator, then a salon area with a couple of bench seats that converted to bunks with the mast in between them, and a little two-cylinder diesel engine in the back. No electronic communications save for a VHF radio, no weather equipment, no computer navigation. Just the wind, the water, and dead reckoning.

"You ready?" George asked.

"Yeah. What do you want me to do?"

"Do you know how to do anything?"

"Still figuring things out," I said.

"If I want something done, I'll tell you to do it, and how I want it done. Untie us from those cleats and we'll get going." There wasn't much traffic in Turtle Cove. Just a few sport fish and sailboats, nothing bigger than 55 feet, nobody in too much of a hurry. Island living.

I did as I was told. George cranked up the engine, the whole thing sounding like a washing machine full of marbles. It coughed black smoke and pushed us along at a snail's pace, but we were at sea and I was building up my days. We were putting Providenciales behind us. Next stop: the Dominican Republic.

"What are you doing?" George asked. I was standing next to him as he held the wheel, and I was trying to do something helpful, like spot reefs or sharks or giant squid or something nautical.

"Just keeping watch," I said.

"I steer the boat and keep watch. You rest," he ordered, pointing to the cabin door below. "I'm on for four hours, and you rest, then you're on for four hours, and I rest. That's how this works."

"I'm not tired yet," I said.

"Enjoy that feeling, because you will be."

I wasn't sure what I was expecting, exactly. Maybe that George would take me under his wing and teach me about sailing, or just tell sea stories or something, but instead, he worked and I rested, and then I worked while he rested. I'd lie on the bunk, my head toward the bow, one arm braced against the mast so that I wouldn't fall onto the deck when the boat would pitch. It wasn't unbearable, but it also wasn't conducive to sleep. Four hours of trying to stay in my bunk, then my turn at the wheel, trying to keep it pointed at the right compass heading. No talking. No stories. Just the wheel, the bench, and the horizon.

We were at sea for a day or so, and then we pulled into our first port, Puerto Plata. A small port city on the north coast of the DR that was frequented by cruisers and yachtsman alike on their way down island. It had all the trappings you would expect of a port city in a third-world country. Everything, and I do mean everything, money could buy. Needless to say, it had its, shall we say, *je ne sais quoi*. Nothing new for seasoned sailors, but I definitely didn't fall into that category . . . yet.

"Stay put," he told me. "I just need to take the boat papers and clear customs."

"No problem," I said.

Puerto Plata was part of the Dominican Republic. When you enter a new country, you have to clear customs. That means the captain takes the paperwork showing where you're from and where you're going, your passports, all the important documents, and gets everything signed off on to clear into the country. While he's doing that, everyone else on the boat, which was me, was in quarantine. I didn't figure George would be gone more than an hour or two.

Or three.

Or four.

After four hours, I started getting really worried. Was there a problem with the papers? Had George gotten hurt? Was he in trouble? Should I leave the boat? If someone stopped me, would that get me into even more trouble? It was basically a banana republic, with soldiers walking around with machine guns, and I didn't want to get caught on the street with no papers and get sent to jail. But maybe I shouldn't have been worrying about George. After all, it was the DR, and they might not have the most efficient bureaucracy, so long delays might just be part of how business was done. I figured that I might as well wait.

Twelve hours later, George finally came back, drunk as hell.

"Where the hell have you been?" I asked.

"Getting us cleared," he said, slurring slightly.

"Everything good?"

"Not a problem in the world," he said. "We're cleared in."

"So, what's next?" I asked.

"Sleep," he said, and basically collapsed on his bunk, unconscious inside of a minute.

The next morning, George woke up drunk, angry, and confused.

"Where's the papers?" he asked.

"What?"

"The boat papers. What did you do with them?"

"I didn't do anything with them. You said last night that you cleared us into the country."

"We still need the papers if we're going to leave."

"So, what did you do with them?"

George looked around, like he hoped he might just spot them sitting on the stove or laying on some charts. Somehow, that didn't solve the problem.

"They have to be someplace," he said.

Yeah, no shit. Unless they'd been completely destroyed, which was entirely possible, they had to be *someplace*. George coming to this realization wasn't exactly progress. Though it may have been in George World.

This was not good news. We were in a foreign country, there were military personnel walking around on the street corners with M-16s, and we had no legal standing and no way to go forward or back.

I asked George to tell me everything he could remember.

Apparently, after getting the papers signed, George decided to celebrate by raising a glass at a local bar. And since anything worth doing is worth doing well in Crazy George world, George then hoisted a few more. George was the kind of guy who kept drinking until he was out of money or the bar ran out of liquor, and this bar had been stocked.

"You're sure you cleared us in?" I asked.

"Positive."

"Great. Let's go to customs."

"Why? I told you we're cleared."

"Because you must have gone to customs to do that. And if you had the papers when you left there, maybe you'll see something in the neighborhood that looks familiar so we can get off this rock. Got it?"

He nodded, but it wasn't the definitive action of a leader who understands the situation and was taking charge. He just nodded because I was talking and he didn't have a clue. Christ, it was going to be on me to grab the rudder and figure this mess out.

I dragged his hungover ass to customs, asked if anything rang a bell. At that point, I would have been surprised if he could have found his own reflection in a mirror.

I was just waiting for George to reveal that he'd lost the boat in a poker game or that he'd accidentally incinerated the paperwork while lighting up a huge joint at a cockfight or some other crazy thing. I'd have believed anything.

Finally, he saw a bar he recognized, a place called Maria's. I can only assume it was named in honor of the Virgin Mother. What really surprised me was that George had been unable to remember where it was, despite the fact that it was just two doors down from a place that should have been all too familiar to George: the police station.

The sight of the police station should have been a good thing. Police, we're told as children, are our friends. But this was a town that didn't pay their police a lot of money, and if we'd gone to them, it would have just been adding more headaches and trouble onto our plate. If the police found out we'd lost the boat papers, they'd either not be able to find them, or they would have, and then asked for a "fee" for their trouble. So no police. I was born at night, but it sure as hell wasn't last night.

It was still early, so I wasn't even sure Maria's would be open, but the door wasn't locked. George liked to frequent the kinds of bars that didn't wait until PM to start serving liquor. The place had a courtyard and a bar and *lots* of bedrooms. So it was pretty much full service. I sure as hell hoped that George hadn't given the boat papers to a hooker after he'd drank away everything in his wallet. I had no intention of paying a wad of cash as a bribe to get back our documents when I was only getting paid $250 for the job. Luckily, George took the lead when we walked in. He was, maybe not surprisingly, a pretty popular guy.

"Morning," George said to the bartender.

"Hey! Mr. Nassau Royale!" the bartender said. George had a fondness for Nassau Royale Liqueur, a popular Bacardi product in the islands. Though, as his nights would go on, he would, like many of us, become less and less particular.

"You remember me?" George asked.

"Sure, mon, de life of de pahty," the bartender said.

This was potentially good news. Not only did he recognize George, but he seemed happy to see him. Maybe George had spent enough money in the place the night before that they wouldn't try to fleece him. Unless he spent so much money that they thought he was an easy mark with a ton of loose cash. Then we were in trouble.

"Did I leave something here?" George asked.

"Oh, yah, mon, to be sure you did," said the bartender. "You asked me to hold on to dese so you wouldn't lose dem." He retrieved some documents from behind the bar, then handed them over to George.

"Appreciate it," George said.

"How 'bout some Nassau Royale dis mornin'?" the bartender asked.

George actually thought about it for a second before saying, "Nah, we should be on our way."

"Suit yourself, mon. Have a good one," he said.

As we were walking out of Maria's, George said, "Hot damn! Left the boat papers at the whorehouse. But got 'em back. Glad *I* got that cleared up." I just looked at him dumbfounded. George was a walking shit show. He said that like it was just one of those things that happens on a daily basis. Not as a major, near-catastrophic fuckup, but just some normal, random thing that happened to people in port. Hell, maybe for George this was just SOP (standard operating procedure). But to me, this wasn't normal, and I didn't want it to become the new normal.

George was one of those guys who managed—reflexively, stupidly, miraculously—to land on his feet every time. He might be pretty unsteady, but on his feet nonetheless. I worried that I didn't have his kind of luck. I'd have to rely on doing things right instead of doing things lucky.

George was determined to make a stop in the city of Samana, on the east coast of the DR. He didn't say why he needed to do it, just that it was something he needed to do. After stopping there, we'd make a run to Puerto Rico, fuel up, and then deliver the *Morgan* to the BVI. It didn't make much sense. Why go to Samana? It would only add time to our trip, and we didn't need any resupply there. I began to suspect that while I was being paid a flat rate for the job, George might be getting paid by the day, and anything he could do to add to our time at sea would only add to his wallet. A tough lesson to learn, but I wasn't going to forget it.

That's when we started getting into some rough weather. Keep in mind, the weather forecasting technology in that part of the world was pretty sparse at that time. We didn't know what we were getting into. But we should have.

It was pretty hairy, but things were starting to calm down when we began to approach Samana. This was back in 1987, and I had a little cassette tape player, a small Walkman, so I could listen to music, because I sure as shit wasn't going to be listening to George impart his wisdom of the seas. I'd been on watch for most of the night, so the sun was just starting to come up. Having some light dispel the blackness of the night, the uncertainty, the chaos, was a tremendous relief. The wind was dying a bit as well, or at least it seemed that way. I looked to the starboard side, and I was overcome with these enormous cliffs, and never in my life had I seen so many palm trees. It was like all the palm trees in the world were gathered on that island as a welcome for us and our tiny sailboat. The combination of the sun chasing away the darkness, the view of those cliffs and those trees, and the sound of "Brothers in Arms" by Dire Straits was just a magical moment for me. This was why I had taken this job. This was why I had wanted to work on the sea. This was what I had come for.

I'll never forget it. All of the ass-beating weather and all of the crap we'd gone through kind of melted away at that point. There's nothing like finding a little island of peace and warmth and light after a cold, dark night to give you a sense of order in the world.

As we were dropping anchor in Samana Bay, I saw another boat that I recognized, a sport fisher from Provo. George and I waved it over and said hello to some friends of mine from Turks and Caicos. Rick, Tom, and Bob greeted us warmly and asked how our sail had gone. George, who knew the guys but not very well, didn't have much to say other than to ask them to drop him off at the dock so he could visit a friend he knew in town. They were happy to comply. To be honest, I was glad to see him go since I was still steamed from having to bail him out in Puerto Plata.

I should have gone into town with George just to keep an eye on him, knowing what kind of trouble he could get into. I should have made some pretense about needing to get some food and supplies, but George had said we didn't need anything, since we got fuel in Puerto Plata, and we had plenty of cold rations on board. Total rookie mistake on my part.

"You guys going to stick around long?" I asked.

"Just passing through," Bob said. "On our way to St. Thomas for a marlin tournament."

The guys were working the billfish circuit (marlin, sailfish, etc.) on the sport fish. It was a hell of a boat. They'd actually placed third in a marlin tournament in Turks and Caicos, which brought them a bonus of about $800 per crewman. Seemed like pretty good money to me, since I was expecting about a third of that for working this job that wasn't going to be nearly as much fun.

"You think you need any extra hands?" I asked, only half-kidding.

"Think you can bait some lines, rig some reels?" Rick asked.

"Piece of cake," I said.

"Hell, if you're near St. Thomas, look us up. The tournament's starting in a few days, and we could always use an extra hand."

"Can you throw some cold soup in to sweeten the deal? I've got a certain lifestyle I've grown accustomed to."

"Hell, we have fully stocked freezers, a full galley. Clean sheets. Air conditioning, warm dry bunks. I think we can find some soup. But first, let's find something to drink!"

Sounded good to me. The next thing I knew, I was with them, walking on dry land, looking to relax in the Dominican Republic.

It was a relief to be off the water. I was still a little queasy from the rough trip into Samana from Puerto Plata, so getting on dry land helped restore calm in my head and my stomach. Maybe we should've gotten something to eat (it had been a day or so since my last hot meal), but first we had to have a few drinks and also a few more drinks. I'd been burning through a ton of calories on this trip and wasn't replacing them as effectively as I should have, what with the lousy rations George had stocked on board (canned soup, beans and franks), so I should have taken it a bit easier on the booze when we got to town. But I needed to warm myself up, I didn't want to be rude, and I was young enough not to know better.

Now, Rick, Tom, and Bob were good people. They weren't trying to start trouble or get chesty with anyone. But sometimes, people can be a little clueless. And Rick was acting a bit more clueless than usual. Maybe it was because he knew a big American sport fish in this little town was a big deal, since it brought a lot of money into the community. With that in mind, Rick seemed to be under the impression that 1) We were doing a lot for Samana by being there; 2) There's no law against having a good time; 3) We were Americans with money to spend, so we probably operated in a state of diplomatic immunity; 4) We're young and can do what we want, and anyone who doesn't understand that should fuck off. So, he had a good amount to drink, arguably (very arguably) to excess. Then he pulled out a big fat joint in the street and just smoked it in plain sight. He probably meant it as "Hey, we're just chilling out and relaxing and it's no big deal," but the message he was sending was "Your stupid island laws don't apply to me." Though, to be fair, we were on a third-world island where laws were loose and selectively enforced.

You know who doesn't take kindly to insults against the law in a banana republic? The law in a banana republic.

In general, on the islands, people give you a wide berth. Things are pretty relaxed and there are few hard-and-fast rules. Instead, there was a more general "ways of doing things" that makes the systems go. The local constabulary wasn't in business to drive potential customers or tourists away, and they tried not to make themselves too conspicuous. That said, if someone was flouting the law, and doing it in a particularly ugly-American way, something had to be said.

We were having a few drinks at a bar, having a pretty good time, maybe having more of a good time than we should have. This was the kind of place where you ordered four rum and Cokes, and they brought you a bowl of ice, one can of Coca-Cola, and a bottle of rum. You'd mix your own, the whole thing cost four dollars, and the most expensive part was the Coke. As we raised our glasses, the local commandant approached us.

He was a big guy, and he knew it, walking with the kind of swagger that showed a lot of confidence in his power, in his authority. He wasn't one of those big guys who acted self-conscious about his size, hunching over to negate his height or putting his hands in his pockets to reduce his bulk. This guy reveled in it. Everything about him announced that he wanted to be seen, wanted to make an impression. He wore camo fatigues, which only seemed more conspicuous in the center of the city. He sported a big mustache and was covered in bangles, the little metal bracelets clinking as he adjusted his belt. Though the accessory that drew far more attention than his jewelry was the gun he wore on his hip, a big revolver I had a tough time taking my eyes off of.

"It's a nice night," he said.

"Very," I replied.

"You all seem to be having a good time," he observed.

I looked around, getting a little nervous. "Yeah, it's a fun town, a fun island."

"It can be. But sometimes, when you have your fun, it's good to move on, before your luck turns bad."

"Is that right?" I asked.

"It's better not to press your luck, you understand?"

I understood very well. He wasn't trying to threaten me. He wasn't saying that me and my friends had to leave or we'd end up hacked to death in the sugarcane fields. But Rick had smoked dope in a public street, and that made the commandant look like an asshole, and so now we had to leave, or there would be a response. Maybe that would mean that the local cops would search Rick's sport fish for contraband, or they'd have their boat papers reviewed and require them to stay in port for a few more days to clear up any red tape, or any of a number of somewhat petty, arguably justified ways of making life unpleasant for us as a way to discourage the kind of behavior that we'd been putting on display.

"I think everyone was planning on leaving before sunup," I said.

"That sounds wise," the commandant said.

My friends agreed, and they decided to set sail at five thirty in the morning. Problem solved. At least, their problem.

I had a new problem.

First, I wasn't sure if the commandant's implied threat applied to only my friends on the sport fish or to me as well. I figured I should just tell George what happened and use his experience and wisdom to divine a course of action.

Problem was he had vanished. Again.

He'd left for town that morning. He'd been gone all morning, and all night as well. I figured he'd be back by midnight, but nothing. Shit, was he hip-deep in a bottle, just like he was in Puerto Plata? Was I going to have to go back into town and find him?

If I was going to have to hunt him down, it was going to have to be after some sleep. I'd been awake at the helm since about two the previous morning, and now I'd been awake, going pretty hard, for over twenty-four hours and was exhausted. And pretty drunk. I decided to get some shut-eye on the *Morgan* and see how the world looked under the light of a new day.

The sun arrived, but George did not. No sign of him in the morning. Or at noon. As nightfall came, and there was still no sign of George, I began to worry. This was supposed to be a quick two-day trip, and we'd been on the hook in Samana Bay for two days now. Damn—I knew that I was going to have to go into town and bail him out, sober him up, or ID his corpse. I fell asleep resolved that if I didn't find his body in some gutter, I'd kill him myself.

I was woken around three in the morning by the sound of something banging against the hull. I grabbed a flashlight and a gaff hook and went to see what was making the noise. I was hoping it was some driftwood bumping into the hull and not someone trying to steal the boat. I raised the hook high.

It was George.

He was sopping wet, apparently from swimming from shore to the boat, and he was totally shitfaced. He might as well have submerged himself in rum and vodka instead of seawater, he was so blitzed.

"George, where the hell have you been?" I asked.

"We've got to go," he said.

"Yeah, we've had to go for the last two days, but I've been waiting for your drunk ass."

"No, we gotta go. Now. We gotta hurry. Look what they did to me!"

His hands were clutched around his leg, and I hadn't noticed at first because of the dark and the fact that he was totally wet, but when I shined the flashlight on his leg, I saw that there was blood everywhere.

"What happened?" I asked, edging a little closer.

"They attacked me!"

"Who?"

"Fucking pirates!"

"You're a fucking pirate."

"We have to go before they kill me!"

I didn't need much convincing. I threw George a first-aid kit, pulled up the anchor, and we headed out of Samana Bay and into the Mona Passage in the dead of night. Not my best move, but I was green and didn't know any better, and my present company was better than nothing. Not by much, but better.

The Mona Passage was where two different currents, and two different wind patterns, converge. It's pretty rare for it to be calm. It's considered to be one of the most difficult passages in the Caribbean. Because apparently, we needed some additional challenges on this journey, and just being saddled with George wasn't enough of a handicap.

Once we were under way, I took a better look at his injury. If we'd been near a hospital, in friendly territory, he could have taken five stitches or so, but we weren't, and he would live, so he could deal with it. Then he told me how he'd gotten the gash or at least his version and what he could recall.

When he got to shore, he'd gotten blind drunk, so his ability to recount details or even reliable time references was compromised, but after he'd had one or two, or ten, he decided to go to a friend's bar, probably in the hopes of getting some free booze. But the bar was closed. And it's possible that the place wasn't even his friend's bar. Hell, it's entirely possible that the place wasn't a bar at all, just the exterior of a hat shop that he *thought* or *believed* or *hoped* was his friend's bar. He knocked on the door. No answer. And like lots of drunk people, his solution to this problem was to make more damn noise. So, he started screaming and pounding on the door, insisting his friend open up. That's when the cops showed up.

Keep in mind, in the Dominican Republic, police don't always wear uniforms. And they don't always carry guns. Sometimes, they just carry machetes. They told George to stop making so much noise, and he told them something along the lines of they should go fuck themselves. If he'd been smart, he would have just apologized and walked away. If he'd been only a little drunk, he might have jawed at the cops a bit before turning tail and running. But this was Crazy George. He didn't stop making noise, and only increased his screaming, now yelling at both the locked door and at the cops for interrupting him. Classic case of "dump truck mouth and wheelbarrow ass."

He became so frustrated that he started kicking the door, trying to force it open, to smash it down to prove, I guess, that he was supposed to be able to get inside. That was the last straw. As he raised his leg to deliver yet another blow to the door, one of the cops unsheathed his machete and gave George a whack, which, in my opinion, he deserved. That's what sent him screaming back to the harbor.

Problem solved, right? Wrong.

Because now it was three in the morning, George was drunk and hurt, and we were going headfirst into what was becoming a pretty severe storm. But we didn't know that at the time. All was calm in the harbor, but it wasn't on the outside, as we were about to find out.

"My leg is fucking killing me!" George said, wrapping it with gauze.

"Good," I said. "Couldn't happen to a nicer guy." If you're going to be dumb, you had better be tough.

It may have sounded pretty cold, but George had gotten himself, and me, into this mess in the first place. He's the one who got drunk and disappeared for two days before getting into a fight with the Dominican cops and almost got me involved with them, too. As far as I was concerned, he needed a little bit of pain for all the bullshit that he was pulling.

My anger at George helped power me into the storm, made me feel like wrestling the wheel could subdue the rain and the wind and the waves. But the angrier I got, the more powerful the storm became. We kept going southeast, through the Mona, and we were getting our asses kicked. The seas were so high, we had to look straight up to see any kind of sky, otherwise it was just waves big as mountain ranges. Day turned to night, and things just got worse. The rain slashing down was like taking a 16-gauge full of rock salt to the face. The waves got higher and steeper, and I felt I might go over the side without a lifeline, so I tied myself in when I was at the wheel. Every half hour, I'd have to lean over the side and throw up. We had to keep the sails down or they'd be torn apart, except for a little reef sail we kept for stability. Our two-cylinder was complaining a lot but still running. We kept pouring oil into it to keep it going, belching smoke the whole way. I didn't know what would happen first—we'd run out of fuel and start drifting or we'd run out of oil, the engine would seize, and then we'd start drifting.

The *Morgan* was taking a pounding, and so was I. A wave would hit the hull, knocking us back, and I'd slam into the gunwale, bruising my knees and hips. I kept jamming my toes against the sides of the cockpit, and worried one would snap, leaving me limping around the deck with one-legged George as my only replacement.

I was wearing foul-weather gear, but it's not like it's a storm-proof vest. Rain and breaking waves were constantly getting flushed out by the scuppers, but I was always ankle deep in water and getting whipped by 35-knot winds. Rain was going sideways, and I just hoped we didn't get hit by lightning. When you're on the crest of a wave, the mast is the highest thing for miles. It's so dark, you can't see which direction the waves are coming from. During the day you can, but at night, it's just an inky void. During day, you can steer the boat into the waves to get a better ride, but at night, you're totally blind, feeling your way through 22-footers.

It was like being in a boxing ring with a blindfold on. You know you're going to get hit, so you tense your body, expecting the blow, but you just never know where the punch is coming from. Then it just slams into you, and you try to recover, knowing there's going to be another one right after that. All night long.

Finally, though, after dark, I finished my watch and was glad to be done with it. My arms and shoulders were sore from wrestling the wheel, partly from the effort of fighting the waves, and partly just from the stress of constantly steeling yourself for the next assault. Your whole body feels like it's been flexing for four hours, and by the end of that watch, I felt like every muscle was ready to cramp up. I needed a break. But there was no leaving the wheel unattended, so I screamed down to George in his bunk.

"You're up!" I hollered.

I was pleasantly surprised when George, either a bit hungover or still half-drunk from the night before, mumbled something incoherent but took his station at the wheel without argument. I took my place on my bunk, resting my hand on the mast to steady myself. Even if I'd be unable to actually sleep during my off-time, it was a tremendous relief to just be able to lie down and have something sheltering me from the wind and the rain. The boat was still pitching pretty hard, and I was exhausted and still feeling sick, but at least I was mostly dry and could recover from the storm for a few hours.

But it wasn't a few hours.

My reprieve lasted just thirty minutes.

George didn't say anything to me, just shuffled over to his bunk, curled up into a ball, and turned his back to me.

"Is it my watch already?" I asked, trying to get a look at my Citizen watch in the dark, not quite making out the numbers.

"I can't deal with this shit right now, so I lashed the wheel down and put out a sea anchor," he said. He'd killed the engine, stuffed a pillow into a 5-gallon bucket, tied it to one of our lines, attached it to the bow, and threw it over the side, making a surprisingly effective sea anchor. The anchor turned the bow of the boat into the waves and held us reasonably in place. We might still drift 20 to 30 miles, but we were still headed toward where we wanted to go.

"George, it's your watch. You've got to steer the boat so we don't drift way off course."

"It's too hairy out there. I'm getting my ass kicked."

"Yeah, for half an hour. I was just out in that shit for four hours, and I didn't punch out early because it was too hairy."

"Then I guess you wish you were the captain. I'm sleeping. See you at first light."

He was right, I did wish I was captain, but that storm taught me that I still had so much I needed to learn, and the lessons would not come easy.

I wanted to reach over there and give him a good bitch slap, maybe even throw him over the side, but that wouldn't help us. I sure as hell wasn't going to spend another four hours at the wheel because George couldn't hack it. He wanted to drift? Fine—we'd drift.

Morning found us feeling lousy and looking worse. The storm had died down a bit, and the sunrise helped, but we were in some sorry shape. After thirty hours of fighting the storm, we had salt sores on our backsides. It wasn't fun to sit, that's for sure, but you sure as hell didn't want to stand. Our asses were chapped as hell. We were tired of being wet, tired of being cold, bruised up and down from slamming into the boat, and George still had his machete injury, which I took a small degree of pleasure in. The good news was that the salt water helped prevent infection. The bad news was that it was salt water in a machete wound, and that wasn't much fun. But George was tough. Hell, when God was handing out brains, George must have been getting second helpings of tough.

No longer requiring the sea anchor, George tried to haul it back into the boat, but a 5-gallon bucket full of water and a waterlogged pillow weighed about 60 pounds, and he had to reel in 200 feet of line against the current. After a couple of minutes of tug-of-war, he turned to me.

"You want to give this a try?" Yeah, like that required a response.

"Not really," I said. Hell, I'd finished *my* watch.

"Yeah, fuck it," he said, unsheathing a knife and cutting the bucket loose.

With the makeshift sea anchor on its way to the bottom, along with 200 feet of really good line, we hoisted the sails and were on our way. The storm had pushed us about 15 miles north of Puerto Rico, adding yet more time to what should have been a short, sweet trip. We should have been a lot closer. For half the day, we worked our way back toward the island.

The boat was as trashed as we were. Everything that was in a cupboard had gone flying across the cabin and cockpit, dishes and silverware flung everywhere across the galley and rest area, and everything was totally wrecked. It looked, appropriately, like we'd been in a hurricane.

We pulled into Puerto Rico to rest and refuel. We were almost there. Just one short run and we could deliver the boat. After we got the fuel and had some cold chicken noodle soup and hot dogs, we spent the next day motor sailing over to the British Virgin Islands.

We straightened up as best we could, got the boat presentable, and finally pulled into Tortola. It was a two-day trip that ended up lasting six days. We'd lost our boat papers, were attacked by machete-wielding police, and survived a hell of a storm. Shame of it was, we weren't getting bonus pay for hazardous duty, or extra pay for stupid duty, so the $250 I was promised for a couple of days' sail didn't look quite so worthwhile after almost a week.

Still, I got my money. And, if you want to look at the experience charitably, I actually got more days at sea, so that was, arguably, worth it.

We picked up our plane tickets in Tortola, though it wasn't first-class accommodations all the way back to Turks and Caicos. It was, like everything else on the trip, the economy package, basically flying standby, with a stop at St. Thomas on the way back. If you were to fly direct, it would be a little over 400 miles. That's about the distance from Boston to DC. But we weren't flying direct.

In St. Thomas, I bid good-bye to Crazy George.

"You're not going back to Provo?" he asked.

"Not with you, George. My buddies from the sport fish said they could use an extra deckhand for their marlin tournament if I was in the neighborhood. Guess I'm in the neighborhood now," I said.

It had been a tough trip, longer and harder than I'd expected. And if I'd wanted to, I could have just continued on my flight back to Provo. But I hadn't taken the job with George because I knew it was going to be a fun vacation. I took the job because I wanted to work on boats. And even though the trip had been one disaster after another, it hadn't changed my mind of what I wanted to do. I loved the challenge of it all. Just that one moment of coming into Puerto Plata with the sun coming up and Dire Straits in my ears was enough to outweigh losing the papers and the storm and all the rest. This trip may have been less an adventure than a misadventure, but it wasn't going to make me change course on what I wanted to do.

"Think they need a captain?" he asked, laughing to himself. A joke that wasn't a joke.

Needless to say, I'd rather drag my dick through ten miles of broken whiskey bottles than set sail with George again. "I think they're good," I said.

"See you around," he said, walking to the waiting area. I headed out to the harbor.

I'd completed the voyage, not nearly as dumb as I was when I started, and I was certainly a great deal tougher for the experience. *I'm learning*, I thought to myself, *albeit the hard way*.

I needed more days quickly.

Chapter 3

Serious as a Heart Attack

The morning had the feel of a Saturday, but then again, when you're living on island time, most days feel like a Saturday. It wasn't like living in New York or Indianapolis or even Fort Lauderdale. On Turks and Caicos Islands, you decide, every day, what you'll do. If you want to go to work, you'll go to work. If you want to go for a swim, then you'll go for a swim. I owned a restaurant, so if I wanted to work that day, I'd open the door, and people would know that I was open for business. And on a day I felt like not going to work, I'd just keep that door closed and find something else to occupy me. On that particular day, it was fishing. It didn't have to be a holiday or a weekend—it just had to be what I wanted to do.

The sky was cloudless, and the ocean was as pristine as the air, the water so clear that it was more like hovering in space than floating on the sea. So immaculate was the water that we could see 50 feet down to where our bait and hooks were waiting, clear enough that if a fish approached that looked too skinny or runty we'd just shake the line to discourage it. We wanted something big, something with some fight to it.

Be careful what you wish for.

The four of us—me and my son Josh and two of his friends, Brian and Mark—were fishing past the reef just off Club Med. We were fishing off a 22-foot center console boat, named *BriMar* after the two boys, that their dad was kind enough to let us use. We used spinning rigs, hoping to catch something delicious.

"That one look good?" Josh asked. He was only eleven but loved every day on the water, just like his old man.

"Nah," I said, wiggling the line to dissuade the fish. "Looks slow and lazy. And small. Let's find one that'll be a decent dinner."

We were fishing for grouper. Now, some of these fish can get huge. The Goliath grouper can be up to 600 pounds and could feed a family of five for two years. We weren't going to hit a strike like that, but we could still get a good 10-pounder. The grouper was one of the ugliest fish you're likely to see, a nasty-looking big-mouth bass. Lots of ugly animals are delicious. Grouper, lobster, monkfish—all incredibly tasty.

"What about that one?" Josh asked. I looked down and saw a good 12-pounder orbiting the bait on his line.

"Yeah, that'll be fine," I said.

The grouper gave it a little more thought, and then he struck, the line going taut.

"Reel him in!" I said.

Josh was excited to get the fish, and so was I, but there was another reason that I felt some immediacy to landing the grouper: barracudas.

There were plenty of barracudas in the waters around Turks and Caicos, and they were basically the hyenas of the sea. They'd wait for someone to catch, kill, or injure a fish, and that's when they'd make their move.

I'd seen it happen up close and personal. I was fishing with my buddy Rusty, hunting for lobster—or, as we called them, bugs—and carrying our Hawaiian slings, these pretty rudimentary spear guns. He spotted a nice-looking mutton snapper and thought it would be an ideal target of opportunity. He took aim and released his sling, the spear going right through the fish. As it was going through its death flop, I got a little closer to get it in my lobster bag. My fingers were just grazing the scales when the fish seemed to convulse, and then there wasn't any fish there anymore. Or, to be more accurate, there was just the head.

I blinked to get my bearings, and then I saw what happened— a big 5-foot barracuda had ripped that fish from me, tore the body loose and left me nothing but the head.

The speed of the attack got my heart rate going. Mentally, I knew I should be okay. The barracuda was big and fast and strong, with fangs like the stalactites of a cave, but they didn't want to eat people. We are not part of their food chain. They operated under the rule of "Attack what you can digest," and a 185-pound man was too much of a meal for even a hefty barracuda. They were just scavengers, and as long as I didn't get between him and his dinner, I should be okay. Unfortunately, if I did get in the way, that fish could take my arm off without much of a sweat. To avoid any confusion, Rusty and I swam to our inflatable and puttered about a mile off, but when we stopped to resume our fishing, that barracuda had followed us. They're fast, can swim close to 50 miles per hour, and our little dingy wasn't going to outrun it. Our day of fishing was done.

This is all to say that I didn't want Josh to lose our dinner to some damn scavenger fish.

"Let's get him up," I said.

The grouper put up a fight, and it was strong, but at about 12 pounds, it wasn't going to require a sport fish chair bolted to the deck and an afternoon of fighting to get him in the boat. After a few minutes, we hauled him in.

Groupers can be fighters. When you get them in a vulnerable position, they'll flare out their gills and all their fins. Dorsal fins will go rigid, their pec fins will stick straight out, and if you're not careful, you could get a close encounter.

Apparently, I wasn't careful.

As Josh swung him into the boat, the fish spun around, and its dorsal fin stabbed me right on the inside of my knee. He kept spinning around, the motion snapping one of those spines right off, leaving it buried in me.

"Damn!" I said, my hand going to my knee. A lot of the time, you get a sharp pain from something, it's just a pinch, just a poke, no big deal. This time, when my hand came back, it came back bloody.

"You okay?" Josh asked.

"No big deal," I said, reaching for some paper towels, wiping the blood away. More blood rushed in to replace what I'd wiped. I wiped at it a little more, figuring it would clot pretty quick, but it just kept going, bleeding down my leg, the blood pooling in my deck shoe. I kept wiping, and it kept bleeding, and pretty soon, I was either going to run out of paper towels, or run out of blood, and neither option seemed ideal.

"Well, hell, this ain't right," I said.

Something was wrong. It wasn't that big of a puncture, so it shouldn't have been causing that much bleeding, but it just wouldn't stop. I didn't know the spine had broken off in my knee, preventing the wound from closing up.

Then it started going numb.

Grouper aren't known for having poisonous spines. So why was my knee losing sensation? There were plenty of things around Turks and Caicos that could poison a fisherman, no doubt. The scorpionfish has spines coated in a powerful toxin that could cause pain, nausea, and paralysis, but those were pretty easy to spot. Stingrays could also spike you with a pretty nasty poison that would hurt, cause nausea, give you fever-like symptoms, and ruin your day. Jellyfish, like a sea wasp, or a Portuguese man of war, could also inflict a pretty nasty sting, but those were fairly easy to avoid. Cone shells were another venomous creature in the water, a kind of poisonous sea snail. They attack their prey with a venom-filled dart containing a powerful neurotoxin that could cause paralysis, respiratory distress, and even death. But they were also mostly nocturnal.

So, what had the grouper hit me with?

There was a chance that the grouper had rubbed up against something that had some kind of toxin on it, or, more likely, the spine from the fish had spiked me near a nerve. Either way, the bleeding wasn't stopping, and the numbness wasn't going away.

Close encounters with sea creatures happened all the time in the islands. Usually, it ended up in a meal. Rarely, you could end up on the receiving end of some pain. Another time when I was out looking for lobsters with my friend Rusty, I'd had a run-in with a shark. We'd collected about eighty lobsters when Rusty spotted a 7-foot nurse shark sleeping in a coral head. He gestured to me that there was more lobster inside that coral. When I went in closer to collect, he jabbed the nurse shark in the ass with his Hawaiian sling and it came flying toward me, slamming into my face and knocking my facemask off. It didn't cause any serious damage, but it sure got my heart going, not to mention making Rusty laugh so hard that he spit the mouthpiece to his snorkel out.

That close encounter ended with just a fat lip and a bruised ego. But this time, I had a limb that wouldn't stop bleeding. This one was serious as a heart attack. Normally, there weren't many situations in a fishing trip that I couldn't fix on my own. I would have liked to stay out and finish the day, but my leg was telling me something else.

Change of plans.

I got ready to make a call. Not on the phone, as the phone system on Turks and Caicos back then was pretty much nonexistent. That, combined with being on the water a lot of the time, meant that we ex-pats relied more heavily on our VHF radios. Portable, dependable, and relatively affordable. I got on the horn to Nancy Logue, the mom of Josh's two friends on the boat, who also happened to be a veterinarian, to see if she could help at all.

Nancy was based in New Jersey, but she loved the islands, and she and her husband, Kenny, a good friend, had bought a house in Turks and Caicos and set up a small veterinary clinic. She'd rotate in a few people when she'd come to visit, a few vets who would be able to spend some time in paradise and, while there, help treat the pets of the islanders. Kind of a working vacation.

On the islands, it seemed that most the ex-pats worked as a working vacation.

"Hi, Lee," she said. "How's the fishing?"

"The fishing's great—just hooked a big one. The boys are all having a blast, and they're all doing well. Wish I could say the same."

"Trouble?" she asked.

I filled her in on what had happened and my current condition. "I'm thinking that maybe I should see Doc Menzie?" I said.

"Let me see if I can get ahold of him," she said. "Get to Turtle Cove, and I'll see if I can set something up so he can take a look at you."

Ewing Menzie was one of the two non-animal doctors on the island. Tall, blond, thin, dapper, and reserved, he was quintessentially British. By the time I'd docked the boat, Nancy got back to me.

"I got in touch with Menzie," she said.

"Should I just go right to his clinic?" I asked.

"If you do, you'll be all by yourself. He's playing tennis at the Yacht Club right now." We may have been in the islands, but we were not totally uncivilized. After all, we did have our Yacht Club, complete with all the amenities.

"What kind of doctor is playing tennis at eleven in the morning?" I asked.

"The kind that doesn't come to work on Saturdays," she replied.

That, at least, answered the question of what day of the week it was. So, it was Saturday after all.

"So where should I go?" I asked. "Is he just going to come by my place for a house call?" Back in the day, it wasn't that uncommon for doctors to actually visit their patients for a house call.

"I'll pick you up and take you to Dr. Faber's office."

"Nancy, there must be some kind of static on the line. Why would I go to Faber's office? The grouper got me in the knee, not the jaw." Dr. Faber was the local dentist, who seemed unsuitable for the task at hand. Not only was I suffering from a pain that wasn't tooth-related, but I knew Faber was off the island, anyway.

"He's not here, but his reclining exam chair still is, and that'll be something we'll need."

Such was the way of things for island living. Nancy was a vet, and a semi-vacationing one at that. Menzie was a proper doctor, but he didn't have an office in a larger, equipment-filled hospital. His clinic was only a few rooms and not set up to treat gunshot wounds or heart attacks or some of the other more serious things that you might encounter at a large, urban hospital. He was more accustomed to sunburns, STDs, dehydration, intoxication, and the bumps and bruises that came with that last condition.

Great. I was going to the dentist's office to get treated by the off-the-clock doc and assisted by the off-the-clock vet. But Nancy was a friend, and I trusted her judgment. On the islands, there was really no such thing as an emergency. The general philosophy when facing some injury or accident was basically that shit happens—now let's just deal with it.

Nancy told me she'd pick me up at Turtle Cove, and she was waiting for us at the dock when we arrived. We told the kids to find their way home, and that we'd see them at dinner, but that plan ran into a lot of resistance. The boys, after all, wanted to keep fishing. They weren't the ones who got stuck in the leg. It might have seemed a little uncaring for them to be so blasé about me having to go to the doctor, but it was, now that I'd learned, a Saturday, and they didn't want their weekend ruined.

They could navigate their way home without any trouble. They were eleven, and it was a small island. Years later, that might be the kind of parenting that would lead Child Protective Services to knock on your door, but in the eighties, on Turks and Caicos, an eleven-year-old could still walk home without it being a horrible case of neglect and abandonment.

I gingerly boarded Nancy's Jeep, a vehicle without roof or doors, designed for island transport, trying as I did to keep the blood off the seats. It would just be lousy form for the island's veterinarian to be driving around in a car covered in blood. It was only a five-minute drive to the dentist's office, but my leg was still bleeding the whole way.

My leg was pretty stiff and numb by the time we arrived at Faber's office. Menzie was already there. He'd apparently come directly from his tennis club, since he was still wearing his tennis whites—white T-shirt, white shorts, white wristbands. It was a good thing he liked tennis instead of golf, because being greeted by a doctor wearing loud checkered pants would have at least *looked* less sanitary.

"Lee," he said, shaking my hand, gazing down at my bloody leg. "What seems to be the trouble?"

Like I said—very British.

They took me into the dentist's office. I don't know if he kept it unlocked while he was away, or if they had access to the key. On the islands, lots of people had a pretty casual unlocked door policy. And what was someone going to do to a dentist's office? Steal three miles of dental floss and five hundred paper bibs? Not very likely.

We didn't have a ton of crime on the island, and the kind we did have was mostly taken care of by letting it take care of itself. If someone got their car stolen, there wasn't going to be an army of CSIs on the scene dusting for fingerprints and analyzing shoe depressions in the sand. It was an island—where was a thief going to go? Pretty much every stolen car was solved the next day when the police or a neighbor would find the car, the gas tank totally drained, abandoned on a beach somewhere. Drugs were a problem, but there wasn't a lot of violence, no gunfire exchanges between rival groups. Some guys just got high, and some guys used their business partner's cash to finance their habit, and everyone would try to live and learn from the experience, but for the most part, there wasn't a lot of crime or a lot of precautions, so getting into Dr. Faber's office wasn't a huge ordeal.

"Have a seat," Menzie said, indicating the dentist's exam chair. I complied.

"You say you got spiked with a grouper's spine?" Menzie asked. I nodded. He looked closely at my knee.

"And your leg is feeling numb? That's not right."

"I'm glad you think so," I said. Always a relief when the doctor believes your paralysis isn't normal.

"Groupers don't have poisoned spines is the thing," Nancy said.

"I was thinking the same thing," I said.

"Doesn't have to be a toxin. Could be that the spine nudged a nerve. Maybe broke off inside the knee. That could account for the bleeding, and the numbness." He tried a few drawers, some of them locked, some of them open, eventually finding what he was looking for—a pair of steel, angled scissors.

"What's that for?" I asked.

"Just in case we need to cut your shorts off," he answered.

"Let's focus on the knee, and not the shorts," I said.

"Suit yourself," Menzie said. He placed the scissors on a table near the chair.

"Don't you want to put that back where you found it?" I asked.

"Your shorts won't be touched, Lee, but your leg is another story. I'm going to have to open it up a bit to see if that spine is still inside." He opened his doctor's bag and removed a scalpel and a few other instruments.

"Can't you just take an X-ray or something to figure that out?" I asked.

"Sure. You know where I can find an X-ray machine on the island?"

He explained that the only way that he would be able to determine if and where that spine might be in my leg was just to go in and poke around. Island living didn't have a lot of diagnostic equipment, apparently.

"That going to hurt?" I asked.

"It's going to be . . . uncomfortable," he said.

Why is it that when doctors are about to do something that will cause you to scream like a little girl, they say, "This is going to be a bit uncomfortable"?

"Can't you give me a shot? Something to numb the leg?"

"If we were in a proper hospital, I probably would, but that's not the sort of thing I usually have on hand. I tried looking for some Novocain, but if Faber has it, it's behind the locked drawers." He once again fished around in his bag a bit before producing a couple of pills.

"Try this," he said.

"What is that? Tylenol?"

"Basically."

That was how we were going to do the surgery. The doctor wearing his tennis whites, being assisted by a veterinarian in shorts and a tank top, cutting into a patient sitting in a dentist's chair medicated with headache pills. That was pretty much island living health care in a nutshell.

He scrubbed up, then put on some rubber gloves. Nancy did the same. I just waited in the chair for the "medication" to take effect. After twenty minutes or so, they started in. It was like getting surgery in the wild west, except instead of a bottle of whiskey, I had a couple of aspirin, instead of a belt to bite down on, I had the vinyl arms of the dentist's chair in a death grip. Piece of cake.

First, they poured some antiseptic on the wound. That let me know that the pills Menzie had given me weren't working nearly as well as I had hoped. I inhaled sharply at the sting.

"Sorry about that," he said.

Why are they always sorry? "Let's just get this over with," I said.

If they had some kind of X-ray, they'd know exactly where to go. But all they had was my bleeding leg as a guide. To find out where the spine was, they just had to go in after it and look around.

From the patient's perspective, it's a hell of a lot more painful looking with your fingers than looking with an X-ray.

Every time they'd stick a scalpel or a retractor into the wound, it felt like they were sticking a hot poker into my leg. Since the spine had stuck me straight in, it made it harder to find. The missing spine would only look like a tiny dot. If they could even see it through the blood. If it was even there. Which required a lot of poking, prodding, and cutting.

It was exploratory surgery with pretty much zero anesthetic, just cutting into the knee until they finally found something hard and sharp that didn't look like part of my knee. But there's lots of things in a knee that are hard, like bone and cartilage and tendons, that don't feel great when you try to pull them out to test whether they're a foreign body. The instruments hurt like hell, but at least they didn't feel excruciating and just *wrong* as the probing fingers, little fleshy worms burrowing into my skin. It must have been less than fifteen minutes, but it felt like hours, each exploration a new level of pain.

Finally, they found it.

"I think that's the culprit," Menzie said, extracting a thin, needlelike spine from my knee.

"Thank Christ," I said, sweat streaming down my face.

"You want to keep it? A souvenir?" he asked.

"The scar will be a good enough reminder," I said.

"Up to you," he said, dropping it in a tray. It made a brittle clinking sound. "Do you have any preferences on the stitches?"

"Just that they be close together and functional, I suppose. How many you think you're going to put in?"

"Maybe a dozen or so? Should be a good story for your wife."

"She loves a good story," I said.

After the final stitch went in, Menzie started putting things back in his bag and found something he wasn't expecting.

"Well, how about that," he said. "It looks like I do have some Demerol. Think you'd want that now?"

They say better late than never, but I wish he'd never have told me that a more thorough inspection of his bag could have saved me a lot of pain on the table.

"No, thanks," I said. "Once the last stitch is in, I like to stop using the painkillers."

"Understandable. Well, we can still use them later."

"For what?" I asked. "Did you find more than one spine up in there?"

"No, I just mean when we take the stitches out. If you want."

"Please, doc. I'll take the stitches out myself. Won't be the first time. Write me a prescription for a beer, and I'm all set."

For stitches, you wanted a steady hand on them putting them in, but anybody could take them out. Just needed to make sure you got them all. Making a separate trip to the doctor just to get rid of some stitches is like going to the doctor to have a Band-Aid removed.

"How much do I owe you?" I asked.

Menzie removed his gloves, looked up at the ceiling while he figured. "Couple of pills, couple of stitches, call it an hour of time . . . how about fifty dollars?"

That's just how medicine worked on the island. No one had insurance. You didn't get referred to ten different specialists. You didn't have to submit a hundred different forms. You saw the doc, he did what he needed to do, he gave you a bill, you paid it. All in all, pretty simple.

"Okay if I drop it off to you on Monday?" I asked.

"When is that?" he asked.

"Day after tomorrow," Nancy said.

"Oh, certainly, that will be fine."

He and Nancy helped put a wrap on my knee over the stitches, and I was good to go.

The next day was Sunday.

A good day for fishing.

Chapter 4

≈≈≈≈≈≈

You Got Your Tit in a Wringer

Surprises at sea are never good things. You keep your eyes open, you listen to your captain and your crewmates, but if something surprising happens, it's usually going to be bad. Broken equipment, injuries, storms, rotten food. All were surprises, none of them good. It never happened that you'd reel something in while fishing and find your hook attached to a chest full of gold coins, or you'd find steaks in the galley instead of bologna sandwiches, or you'd make a four-day sail in twenty-four hours. If something good was going to happen, you'd know about it a mile off. The things that were able to find you without any warning—that was never going to be good news.

"We've got company," Rick said, pointing beyond our stern.

Hadn't expected that.

We were on our first day of a four-day sail to Nassau. Rick was the man in charge of our four-man crew. He was the same guy who'd owned the sport fish that I'd abandoned Crazy George to go work on. He knew what he was doing, that's for sure. It was a pretty straightforward operation. The owner of the boat, Alex, had hired me and three other guys to sail it from Turks and Caicos to Nassau as a way to save some money. For luxury goods, like a sailboat, the cost of declaring residency in a country was a duty that could be 75 percent to 100 percent the cost of the luxury good. So, a $500,000 sailboat spending a year in port would merit duty of up to half a million dollars. But there was a pretty easy workaround to avoiding this crippling tax—go on a weeklong sail.

Maybe the original intention behind the law was to get nomads and wanderers to move to other places, but in legal terms, a boat owner could just sail away from Turks and Caicos, clear in to a foreign port, come right back, and they would manage to avoid the hefty duty. And hell, the owner didn't even need to be on board when he made the sail—he could just hire a crew to do it for him. That's why I was on board to begin with. Just help three other guys sail the boat into Nassau and come back, and we'd each collect $400 for a week's work. Not too bad.

Unless you ran into any surprises along the way.

The boat itself, *Southern Nights*, was absolutely gorgeous. It was a 60-foot Formosa, a twin-masted ketch made in Taiwan with a couple of beautiful hand-varnished wooden masts. The whole boat was just immaculate. Keeping a boat like that in ship-shape required a lot of maintenance. It was amazing to look at and pretty damned comfortable to boot. But it wasn't made for speed, and there was no way that we were going to outrun what was quickly gaining on us.

The Coast Guard.

It was a medium-sized boat, maybe 150 to 170 feet long, probably a Sentinel-class (Fast Response) cutter. Those boats could boogie to the tune of almost 30 knots, featuring four officers and twenty crew. And just to keep everyone honest, it had four crew-served Browning M2 machine guns, capable of spewing out six hundred rounds of .50-caliber ammo per minute, and a Mark 38 Model 2.25-mm autocannon.

"Where did they come from?" I asked Rick.

"That's how they operate. They come at you from behind, every time. Keep you on the defensive."

"Yeah, but we're not an enemy cruiser sneaking through the Gulf of Tonkin."

Rick just shrugged his shoulders. "Could just be routine." Rick was a pretty laid-back guy, which wasn't surprising since we all knew our jobs and he wasn't captaining the *Bounty*. Having the Coast Guard behind us worried me, but it didn't seem to cause him much concern.

It wasn't uncommon, certainly. Coast Guard cutters made stops and inspections all the time. It didn't mean that they were specifically looking for us. But it sure as hell didn't mean that was off the table, either.

Our radio came crackling to life.

"*Southern Nights*, this is the Coast Guard. Lower your sail, reduce speed to under five knots, make your course one-eighty, and prepare to receive a boarding party for a safety inspection."

Rick acknowledged the order and confirmed he would comply.

"It's always a safety inspection," he told me, rolling his eyes. How much safety did a sailboat require? Were they going to force us all to wear life preservers and stop running with scissors?

We sprang to action, lowering the sails and getting the diesel going, moving the boat to under 5 knots. I asked Rick why they hadn't told us to cut all power and come to a dead stop.

"It's not a traffic stop on the freeway. Boats just floating around, vulnerable to currents and waves, are a lot harder to board than ones moving at a constant rate of speed." Made sense.

The boat's owner, Alex, hadn't *seemed* untrustworthy. Alex was an expat, like me. The idea of a rich boat owner conjures up images of a tall, blond athlete in Brooks Brothers suits, but Alex was a fairly average-looking guy, a little on the shifty side. He was a bit stocky, seemed to have a few rough edges to him. Maybe that's why he had decided to marry his wife, Louisa, who always caught the attention of every eyeball in the room. She was a smoking-hot blond trophy wife. I figured, that's the reason he'd married her—because she would smooth out his edges. He wasn't really in her league. He was certainly no Don Juan. She was friendly in a Southern way, and I got the impression that she was from Alabama. Maybe that's why he decided to name the yacht *Southern Nights*.

Alex hadn't talked a lot about what he did or what he used to do. He just claimed that he was mostly retired and had come to the islands without a lot of baggage but hauling a ton of money. This hadn't raised too many eyebrows. Hell, back then, the island was full of guys like that, men with skinny bios and fat wallets. For a good chunk of the expats there, everybody was running from something. Maybe it was a failed business, or some problem with the law, or family that was trouble, but you didn't have to leave America for a foreign island if all you wanted to find was sunshine.

Whatever he had left, whatever he was running from, money wasn't a problem for him. He'd built a two-story house overlooking Grace Bay with a swimming pool that was practically linked to the beach out front. The cost of building that setup was about the same price per square foot as a plane ticket from LA to Paris, so it sure as hell wasn't cheap.

Alex may have claimed to have been retired, but he didn't just want to sit on the beach all day and sip piña coladas. He bought into a small hotel, a hundred-room concern right on the beach. Back then, there was a huge French Canadian contingent on Turks and Caicos. The French owned the Club Med on the island, Club Turquoise, a place so exclusive that it had its own time zone. Kind of amazing that an island that was only 17 miles long somehow required two time zones, but that's how it was. There just seems to be something about speaking French that makes people arrogant and standoffish.

Still, for a while, that time difference had helped me when I was in the restaurant business. I'd get a call from the club's food and beverage manager telling me that they'd closed their operations, locking their doors when the clock struck 11:00, and that I should expect a busload of customers because it was only 10:00 where I was. Five miles away, one-hour time difference, and a world apart. Still, the Canadians and the French seemed to love Turks and Caicos, and that's why Alex had wanted to get involved in the hotel. The way he bought in? Cash.

One of the nice things about island living was a streamlined approach to regulation. There just wasn't a lot of oversight. In most places, if you wanted to make a cash deposit at a bank for over $10,000, the bank was required to ascertain the identity of the depositor and report the deposit. That wasn't the way it worked in Turks and Caicos. Whether it was greed or naïveté, banks didn't discourage people from making large deposits. You could bring a half-million dollars in cash inside a suitcase, and the only question you might get asked was the brand of the suitcase.

Of course, that kind of relaxed attitude had a tendency to attract the wrong kind of people. And that kind of people had a tendency to attract the Coast Guard.

I wondered if the Coast Guard cutter might just pull alongside our boat and lay a gangplank across to us for boarding, but they were more militarily efficient. The cutter stayed at our aft, guns trained on us the entire time, while a small Zodiac inflatable launched from their boat loaded with sailors.

"Ahoy there!" the lieutenant in charge of the boarding party said to us.

"Ahoy yourself," I replied.

"Catch our lines," he said.

"You need directions or something?" I responded.

"Just making a standard safety inspection," he said.

We caught their lines and tied them off to the lee side of our boat. Didn't see as we had much choice. He hauled himself on board.

"You want a tour of the boat?" I asked.

"Actually, it might be easier if we have everyone up on deck. We can find our own way," he said.

I nodded.

A half dozen Coast Guard sailors boarded *Southern Nights*, all looking loaded for bear. Flak jackets and M-16s.

"Anybody carrying any weapons?" the lieutenant asked.

We all had pocketknives, but that wasn't what he wanted. Nobody was armed.

Sure didn't sound like the kind of thing that you'd ask during a routine safety inspection.

The lieutenant directed four sailors to watch all of us, then he went down below with a couple of his men.

"Think this'll take long?" I asked the sailor watching me. "Watching" wasn't quite accurate; "guarding" may have been more precise. The guy was big, over six foot, and though the flak jacket added some bulk, I could tell he probably tipped the scales at over 200 pounds.

He shrugged his shoulders in reply.

"Hey, Al," I said to the oldest guy that I'd been working with, "this happen to you a lot for this kind of job?"

"No talking," the sailor in front of me said.

This was looking less and less routine.

It only took a few minutes before the lieutenant returned topside.

"You boys are in a lot of trouble. You know you've got a concealed compartment on board?"

Just a simple little weeklong cruise was now: we were fucked.

Note to aspiring sailors: when a platoon of armed Coast Guardsmen boards your boat, you know you got your tit in a wringer.

For a guy with tons of spare cash, with enough scratch to afford such a beautiful boat and an amazing house and the medical science that helped perfect his wife, Alex had apparently gotten us into this mess because of his cheapness.

The man hadn't been content with just one gorgeous boat—he wanted to buy another one. There was a 55-foot Sea Ray that he had his eye on. He made it clear that he wanted to make an offer, so the owner of that boat called in a surveyor.

A surveyor is an expert at determining the value of a boat. Basically, a surveyor is an appraiser. The owner of the Sea Ray wanted to know how much he should be asking for it during any negotiations with Alex, so he contacted the guy he wanted to use, flew him in to Turks and Caicos, and had him do the job. Simple.

But not quite so simple.

Alex wanted to get *Southern Nights* appraised, too. That's something you do for insurance, or in case he wanted to try to sell it, and so on. And the surveyor that his friend had originally hired was good, too. Maybe too good. He was so competent and knowledgeable that, when inspecting the boat, he knew every inch of what that Formosa was supposed to look like. He knew every board, every line, every hatch. So, when he inspected the forward head, he knew there was supposed to be a bathtub there. That's what that kind of sailboat was supposed to feature. But instead of a bathtub, he only saw a mirror. And, to that surveyor, that didn't make much sense.

Why would you remove a bathtub, and the space it occupied, to install a bulkhead with a mirror on it? It was a red flag, for sure. If an owner modified his boat in a way that did not enhance its value, then that was suspicious. And this surveyor had incentive to be suspicious.

One of the Coast Guard's mandates was fighting drugs. They'd run patrols and monitor air and sea traffic, but they also wanted to get regular citizens involved on their side, so they made people an offer. If someone were to turn snitch and report something suspicious about an asset, something like a car or a house or a boat, then that person was entitled to 10 percent of the value of that asset (after sale at auction). That beautiful Formosa was valued at about a half-million dollars, even in 1985. That meant that an enterprising surveyor could earn himself an extra $50,000 just by making a single phone call. And that's exactly what he did.

Which meant that me and my three crewmates were nose-to-muzzle with a boatload of Coast Guard sailors because our boss decided that he needed to save a couple of hundred bucks on a plane ticket. He didn't have to put himself, or his boat, at risk. He could have just made a call to a surveyor that he knew and trusted and said, "Hey, get down here to Turks and Caicos. I'll double your fee if you sign off on the dotted line without inspecting too closely." It happened all the time. Bribes, kickbacks, generous gratuities—whatever you wanted to call it—it would have still been a hell of a lot cheaper for Alex than losing a boat. But some guys liked to cut corners. Some guys liked the thrill of trying to play an angle. That's probably why he decided to convert *Southern Nights* into a drug boat in the first place.

He probably thought he was being really clever. The swabbies from the Coast Guard told us how it worked. There was a tiny hole behind the toilet paper in the head, which, when probed, would release magnets that would open the secret compartment. It was a great place to stash some Mary Jane. All very smart and clever. Had it not been for the surveyor, they probably would never have caught it.

And because of all that cleverness, my crewmates and I were now looking at twenty years in jail if they found anything in that compartment.

"You guys find anything down there?" I asked.

"Not yet," the lieutenant said.

"Maybe the guy just used that to store his porn," I said.

"Could be."

"So, you didn't find anything. Does that mean we can go now?"

"Nope," he said, nodding his head toward his cutter. A team of sailors was lining up to come on board *Southern Nights*, carrying crowbars, knives, and chainsaws. "It just means that we're going to start looking a little harder."

Damn.

Drugs were a problem on the island. On the one hand, there was plenty to do: swim, fish, sail, explore. But there was also a lot that you couldn't do. In 1985, there wasn't a lot of television. The most sophisticated gaming devices stateside were Ataris and Commodore 64s, and besides what they lacked in advanced graphics, they also lacked in not actually being on the island. So, after swimming and fishing a bit, some people enjoyed the sun a bit more or had a bite to eat, and some people tried to stimulate themselves in other ways. Even in paradise, things can get old.

It was, in many ways, kind of miraculous, because on Turks and Caicos, if you couldn't find drugs, *they would come to visit you all on their own*! One time, there was some treetop flier, some dope runner bound for Florida or Jamaica or some other place, and he got chased by a Coast Guard interdiction jet. Those drug planes weren't made for speed, so this ace just dropped his load and tried to get out of there, and that meant that a bunch of bales of plastic-wrapped cocaine ended up washing onto the beach in Turks and Caicos.

For a lot of islanders, Christmas came early (or late—time was, as always, relative on the island). People grabbed as much cocaine as they could carry and buried it in their yards. It wasn't really considered a horrible taboo to do drugs, but it also wasn't something anyone wanted to just flaunt, and as a result, people started using it openly, but subtly, by stashing the cocaine in empty canisters of nasal spray.

These nasal sprays were small containers that people would traditionally use to clear clogged and congested nasal passages when suffering from colds, flus, or allergies. And while cold and flu season on a tropical island wasn't quite as long as in places like Minneapolis or Chicago, you'd have thought that the entire island was in the midst of some kind of outbreak from the number of nasal sprays being deployed on every street. People would fill their little bottles with coke and then, when they wanted a little toot, just take out their nasal spray and do a bump right there. Though, in all fairness, it probably *did* help clear blocked nasal passages, I'd guess.

I even once saw a guy at a bar carrying a baby's bottle full of cocaine, where he'd cut the top off, and just sprinkled coke right on the bar to do lines. That kind of brazen use was unusual, certainly, and if done by an expat would have resulted in a rapid one-way trip home, but this is to say that drugs were an issue on the island (as I'd experienced firsthand with my old business partner during my days as a restaurateur), and smugglers were a problem. But I wasn't a smuggler—I was just a guy working a job for a little cash.

I just wasn't sure the Coast Guard knew that.

The first few hours, there was nothing to say, and the boat was divided into two crews. One group were the Coast Guard sailors working belowdeck, ripping it to pieces, slicing through mattresses, cutting through bulkheads, prying out fixtures looking for contraband. The other group was topside, a set of armed men keeping an eye on me and the other three guys hired to sail the boat to Nassau. Action below, inaction above. We could hear the sounds of the crowbars, the creak of wood before it splintered apart, and every sound was terrifying, since every creak, tear, and crack told the story of another piece of the ship ripped apart to reveal . . . something. Maybe nothing. But if they found *anything*, then it would mean the difference between us being treated like dumb lackeys and us being treated like known drug smugglers.

As they were ripping it up, I thought it was a shame that they'd have to destroy all of Alex's personal things, all his photos and keepsakes. But the more I thought about it, in those hours as they tore it apart, the more I realized that I hadn't seen anything like that. No pictures of Alex holding up a 50-pound tuna. No photos of Alex and Louisa posing for the camera in front of a beautiful island sunset. No images of any friends or family enjoying the day on a gorgeous boat. For a guy living the life, he was pretty camera shy. This was not a man who wanted people to know his face. And yet, this boat, *Southern Nights*, was where he'd lived for the first few months in Turks and Caicos while he was having his house built. This was his home. But it was a place that seemed as clean as it was anonymous, as immaculate as it was empty. No fingerprint smudges on the hand-polished wood, and that was apparently for good reasons.

After a few hours of work below, silence above, they took a break, and the sailors brought out food from their galley for everyone. It wasn't anything fancy, but it was good; sandwiches and something to wash it down with.

"What was the name of the guy who hired you?" the lieutenant asked.

"Alex," I said. No use protecting the guy. I wasn't part of his posse, I wasn't some foot soldier for his operation sworn to silence. I was just a guy hired to do a job by someone who didn't explain the whole story, and who brought a lot more risk to the table than I was prepared for. All for $50 a day.

"Alex? Nah, that's not right. This Alex is actually Marty," he said. That made sense. He looked like a Marty.

"Where were you headed?" he asked.

"Nassau," I said.

He nodded. He knew the answer before he asked the question. He wasn't trying to get information from me; he was just trying to see if I was holding anything back. I wasn't.

"We're not involved in this," I said, gesturing to the other guys.

"Not for me to say," the lieutenant replied, taking a bite of his sandwich.

"We're just taking the boat from one island to another island."

"Okay."

"We're not drug smugglers."

"You know how I know if you're drug smugglers?" he asked.

"How?"

"If we find any drugs on board, then you're drug smugglers."

I thought to that day on the island where every native was walking around with a nasal spray bottle full of cocaine. Guys would just keep one of those in their pockets, like they were Tic Tacs. What happened if Alex/Marty had something like that? A little, insignificant bottle hidden away in the medicine cabinet or the first aid kit and forgotten? What if they found something like that?

"How many years if you find something?" I asked.

He shrugged his shoulders. "I'm not a lawyer. But at least a year. As much as ten for a first offense, I'd think. So far, it looks empty, but we found one hidden cache, so there's no reason there can't be more."

"Thanks," I said. "Where are we headed?" I could tell we were moving west, but there were lots of places in that direction.

"Miami. Get comfortable."

It was about 180 miles to Miami. At the pace we were going, another two or three days at sea while they ripped the boat to pieces looking for evidence to use to send me to jail for a decade.

I kept eating my sandwich, even though I didn't have much of an appetite.

It was slow going. The cutter could move faster than we could, but they weren't about to give up their prime position behind us to try to tow us in. They were just guys doing their jobs, and I understood that. At the same time, I got a bit of a kick knowing that their boat was one lousy ride. Coast Guard cutters don't ride worth a shit. They're built for speed, built to knife through the water. To reduce drag and weight, they're built long and narrow, which meant that they keep stable by going fast. When going at a snail's pace to keep up with us, that boat had to be rocking and rolling all over the place. The sailors on board had to be pissing and moaning the whole way to Miami. Suck it up, cupcake.

The more time they were looking, and finding nothing, the more relaxed I started to feel. These guys weren't missing anything, judging by the sound of the wood cracking and metal popping. They were thorough. Since they weren't hitting pay dirt, we relaxed a bit, and that helped the tension ease some more.

One sign that things are going in the right direction: when the men put in charge of holding you at gunpoint start talking shit about the boss. The CO of the boat spent most of his time on the cutter, but every now and then he'd visit *Southern Nights* and check in. The lieutenant would call him "Charlie Oscar," since he was the CO. So, I started calling him Oscar Mayer. It got a good laugh, at least when the CO had left. He wasn't a hard-ass, but he was the boss, and everyone's sphincter would pucker a bit more when he was on deck. He wouldn't linger, and when he'd return to his boat, everyone's posture slumped about two degrees.

"He riding you hard?" I asked.

"Not too bad," the lieutenant said. "Though he doesn't always go by the book."

"That right?"

"You know, back when we were patrolling the US Virgin Islands, we used to make a special stop at St. Thomas, just to replenish the supplies of his favorite ice cream."

"No shit?"

"No shit. The man just loves his Butter Brickle."

The Coast Guard patrolling the Virgin Islands makes special ice cream stops to appease the CO's sweet tooth? No wonder the navy likes to make fun of them for being soft.

Still, it was nice to know that they weren't hanging us from a yardarm or preparing to keelhaul us, or whatever the Coast Guard typically did to guys they really think were guilty of drug smuggling. I let out my breath in a sigh. We might make it out of this yet.

It took three days for us to get to Miami, and we finally pulled into port at daybreak. I spent the night trying to rest, but having trouble making it happen. It's kind of hard to sleep when you know that nothing good is coming around the corner. Every little thing wakes your ass up, but you're in the middle of the ocean. You can't just go to the front desk and change rooms. The Coast Guard didn't find any new caches, didn't find any illicit nasal spray, so they didn't slap the cuffs on. It was an uneasy passage, but not torturous. We got three squares a day as we made our way, bacon and grits in the morning, sandwiches for lunch, burgers for dinner. It was better than what we had stocked in our galley. Though, to be honest, I'd have preferred to avoid the whole situation, even if it had cost me a few good meals.

They took us to the Miami Coast Guard station for interrogations, three investigators doing the work. I'd expected heavyset guys in bad suits and aggressive mustaches, but the Coast Guard didn't work that way. Instead, the investigators all wore khaki uniforms with razor-sharp creases. I'd seen enough detective shows to expect some version of good cop/bad cop, but that's not the way that real interrogations work. They weren't trying to trick us into a confession. They made no effort to goad us into some kind of confrontation. They just wanted to get us talking. So, they asked me how I knew Alex/Marty, how I got hired for the job, how we all made our way toward Nassau. And after I told them my story? I'd have to retell it. Over and over and over again. They were looking for inconsistencies, things that I might screw up if I was making things up. Lies can be easy to tell, but hard to keep track of. The truth might sometimes be plain, but it was a lot more memorable.

"How'd you get the job?"

"Marty asked if I'd be interested in a week's work."

"Wait—how'd you know his name was Marty? Earlier, you said you just knew him as Alex."

"What? I don't know. I think the lieutenant on the cutter said his name was Marty."

"Sure, sure."

And over and over again.

"You going to be bringing Alex here to join us?" I asked. "I wouldn't mind telling him what I think about using us like he did."

"That dude is long gone. We knocked on his door right after we picked you guys up, but he's out of here." No sign of him remained. Nothing at his house, nothing at his business. He heard that someone was coming for him, and he and his wife disappeared. I couldn't get any details from them, since they were paid to get information and not give it away. But I was curious if he just blew town or if he was able to get his business partners to buy him out. Not that I felt a lot of pity for him. Not only did he get me parked in a Miami interrogation room, but he did it for the world's dumbest, most avoidable reasons. If he'd paid a few hundred bucks to his own surveyor, he wouldn't have lost his boat, wouldn't have had to abandon his house. So, it ended up saving him a few hundred bucks for a plane ticket but costing him a couple of million in what he had to leave behind.

Marty was clearly no genius for dealing, but the Coast Guard wasn't going to be winning a Nobel Prize for crime fighting any time soon, either. They knew we were nothing, just a few sailors working a job. The guy they really wanted was Marty. So, why'd they board us on day one out of Provo? If they really had wanted to catch him, they would have waited until we returned to Turks and Caicos and then made their move. I guess they got the call from the surveyor and thought they'd bust a nut if they didn't get a cutter dispatched ASAP, but they'd committed the cardinal sin of fishing by scaring off the big fish so they could grab a few minnows. All in a day's work, I suppose.

After about ten hours of the same story told the same way, half a day that felt like fifteen years, we finally heard those magic words.

"You're free to go," our interrogator said.

It was a relief to be free—but now what? I didn't live in Miami. I didn't have a car in town. I'd come in on a boat that wasn't going to be taking me back home anytime soon. Walking outside was like getting out of prison after a ten-year stretch. The Coast Guard had taken our transportation and moved us to a new city, and if it helped us at all, they'd be happy to call us a cab. Provided, of course, that we had cash for the fare.

Luckily, one of our crew, Richard, had an apartment and a roommate in Fort Lauderdale who was able to give us a lift. He took us to his place so we could decompress for a little while. There I was able to call my wife and tell her what had happened. Though we didn't actually have a phone in Provo, so I didn't call her directly. I called my friend Kenny, who was married to Nancy, the vet who had taken the grouper spine out of my leg. I gave him the short version of what had happened, told him to tell my wife I was fine and wouldn't be going to federal prison for a decade and that I'd be back home on Monday. He made sure the info was relayed to her via the coconut telegraph. It was Saturday when we finally got out of holding, and I was able to attend a Miami Dolphins home game the next day. We had a few beers, shot the shit, then tried to move on.

Finally, on Monday, I got a flight back to the island. The whole episode was a real screw job. Not only did I get the Coast Guard detour, but I also had to buy a plane ticket from Miami to Provo. And because I wasn't a native islander, I had to buy a round-trip ticket, paying double for a ticket I didn't even want in the first place! At least I got paid. None of the other guys could say that. I'd been stiffed the previous two jobs I'd worked, and so I'd made sure this time that I got the money up front and in full. The other three guys all got burned.

When I finally got to see Mary Anne, she made it clear that the rumor mill had been working overtime. The entire island seemed to know about what had happened, or at least some version of it. Everyone knew that Alex/Marty was gone, but the details morphed with every telling of the story. Alex's boat was seized by the Coast Guard carrying two tons of cocaine; Alex's boat was full of one hundred bricks of marijuana and an arsenal of guns; Alex was killed in a standoff with the DEA; Alex was Pablo Escobar, he was D. B. Cooper; I was sentenced to twenty years for running drugs; I was shot dead by the FBI during a raid on my compound in Miami.

It starts out as life, but it always becomes a sailor's story.

Chapter 5

≈≈≈≈≈≈≈≈≈

A Good Sailor Never Learned Anything in Calm Seas or Tied to the Dock

Y ou can drown in an inch of water.

It doesn't have to be in the bowels of the USS *Indianapolis* or the bottom of the Marianas Trench. There's no requirement that the water be deep in order for it to be life-or-death. You forget that, you can find yourself in a world of hurt.

I was sailing to the Dry Tortugas with my son Josh and my friends Rick and Little Bobby. We were on a little 40-foot sailboat called *Rickshaw*, a 1970 raised pilothouse ketch, planning to do some weekend fishing. We were headed to a spot 80 miles west of Key West, a place where the water only got to be about 20 feet deep, so the big boats wouldn't want to go. For boats of that size, shallow water could be dangerous. Turns out, they could be dangerous for pretty much anyone.

Aside from the fishing, one of the main reasons that I wanted to make the trip was to visit Fort Jefferson. When you're a sailor, you're naturally attracted to a pirate-like lifestyle, and Fort Jefferson appealed to a piratical nature. The fort was created as a strategic asset to protect the shipping lanes to America's southeast. It's the largest brick masonry structure in the Americas. With Fort Jefferson there, Napoleon or any pirates of the Caribbean couldn't get any ambitious ideas.

Later, the fort became a prison, primarily for Union deserters during the Civil War, where it was nicknamed Devil's Island. Its most famous resident was Dr. Samuel Mudd, the doctor who set John Wilkes Boothe's broken leg after he shot Lincoln. It was quite a sight, and I was hoping Josh would find it interesting. If Rick and Little Bobby found it interesting, then that was okay, too.

I'd known Rick from Turks and Caicos and had fished with him on his sport fish named *Mombo* when I'd parted ways with Crazy George. Both George and Turks and Caicos were now a melancholy memory. After running out of cash, we'd had to sell what we could and move in with my sister Vickie in Michigan.

Michigan wasn't exactly the epicenter for a career in boats, but I didn't have much choice. I needed to get back to the water, but before I could, I needed to build a bit of a bankroll first. Technically speaking, the Great Lakes counted as water. They would work in a pinch. It just wasn't the place where I wanted to live the rest of my life. If you're in a place where you don't want to be, you have two choices: find a way to like what you don't like or find a way to move. I was going to find a way back to where I wanted to be.

My wife, Mary Anne, picked up work as a waitress, and I got a job as a short-order cook. We saved what we could until we had enough money to move to Florida. After moving expenses were paid, all that was left over was about $50, and that would be enough to stave off starvation for about a week. That's how long we had to find ourselves jobs. So that's exactly what we did—Mary Anne took a job waitressing at Skipper's Galley, and I found work at Matanzas Seafarer Company, waiting tables, tending bar, and eventually managing. It wasn't ideal, but sometimes you just have to take what you can to pay the bills. Some people refuse to ever compromise, refuse to pay their dues before their dreams come true. It's a lot like refusing to get in the starting blocks because all you want to do is break the tape at the finish line. Part of being able to cross that line is first hunkering down in the blocks. It would do until something better came along.

With a little time and hard work, something better came along.

I took whatever moonlighting work I could find on boats. Work as a mate on sailboats, work as a first officer on casino boats, whatever I could to build up my hours and make a little money. Eventually, I was able to get my 25-ton license. But if you're going to have a license, then you need to be the captain of something.

That's when I struck up a deal with Rick.

"Feeling a little thirsty," Rick said, his eyes on the horizon.

"What're you in the mood for? Rum or beer?"

It was a guys' weekend, just the four of us sailing and fishing and drinking and telling lies. And probably not always using the best judgment, but that was always something that, assuming things didn't go completely wrong, could be fixed in the telling of the stories.

"Let's start with beer and go from there," Rick said. I reached into the cooler and tossed him a cold one.

I'd known Rick from the islands, but we reconnected in Florida. He had a big sport fish he'd use, but he also had *Rickshaw*, this little 40-footer that was just wasting away. I made him an offer: I'd get her into shape, put in the time and the money and the sweat and get her cleaned up, and in exchange, I'd be able to use *Rickshaw*. He'd still own the boat, and when I was done, he'd have all the benefits of my improvements: scraped-down hull, decks done, varnish work done, sails mended, new stove, new interior. So the boat was Rick's, but it was also kind of mine.

It actually benefitted Rick in two ways. First, he got his boat cleaned up. But second, he got the boat used. Boats aren't like baseball cards or comic books that increase in value by staying in mint condition. A boat is more like the human body, where it functions at a higher level if it is used more. Taking a boat into open water helps keep it from rotting away. Same way with cars. Some guys would buy a classic car and keep it in the garage all year round, only taking it out once in the summer for a car show. That's a great way to keep mud off the fenders, but it's also a great way to let sediment in the gas lines and transform a piece of fast-moving machinery into a giant, motionless block of metal. Some things work better when they're put to use. Men at sea fall into that category, as well.

It was a good arrangement we had. I'd pay for repairs to get *Rickshaw* shipshape, and in exchange, I got to use it for day charters. I didn't have a business degree or a ten-point plan or advanced metrics. All I had was a handmade sign that said "Day Sails," then I'd sit on the beach. Interested folks would come up, hand me some cash, and I'd row them out in my dingy to *Rick-*

shaw, anchored a little ways offshore. Doing those day charters was a great way to build up my hours, but it was also an amazing way to get to know people.

The ocean has a great equalizing effect. When you're on the water, it doesn't matter if you've got a ton of money. It doesn't matter if you're beautiful or ugly, it doesn't matter what kind of car you drive or in what neighborhood you live or where you went to school. When you're out there, all that matters is how well you can get the job done. It's a true meritocracy. If you know the sea and you know your boat, you can have a good day. If you haven't done the work and don't know how it all goes together, you're going to fail, and the ocean can be very unforgiving.

Part of being the captain is being able to read people. When you run a day charter, you have to know how to sail, but if you're going to be able to deliver a good time, you also need to understand, very quickly, what your customers want and find a way to deliver that. Some people want to feel the wind in their hair and the spray on their faces, they want velocity and hard turns.

But that doesn't go for everyone. Some people want the exact opposite. Some people want to just laze around in the sun a half mile offshore, to look back on the beach and think, "I'm getting away from it all . . . but not too far." Those people want quiet, stability, and safety. You have to be able to identify those needs quickly. And you can't just ask them.

It's like the waiter at an Indian restaurant asking a guy how spicy he wants his food. Some guys would ask for the hottest food imaginable just to impress the rest of the table. Similarly, if you ask some guys what they want from a sail, they'll say they want big waves and giant squid and pirates boarding the quarterdeck.

But that might just be what they think their friends want to hear, or what they think they need. You have to read them, to interpret them, to find out what they really want.

I'd see who in a couple was in charge, identify who was the alpha and who was the beta, see who wanted to be pleased and notice who lived to please others. I'd watch how people got on the boat, which ones stepped confidently over the gunwale and which ones jumped in a panic onto the deck, terrified of the gap between the dock and the boat. I'd be aware of the guys who would wear some souvenir captain's hat they bought in a tourist trap and under no circumstances wanted to encounter a situation hairy enough to knock it off their heads. I'd observe the women who'd removed their jewelry beforehand because they were desperate to let their hair down and the ones who didn't want a single hair displaced. There's a lot you can learn from a handshake. A firm grip might indicate that person is ready to lend a hand, and an uncalloused, dead-fish handshake wouldn't possibly be interested in raising a sail or taking the tiller.

I was once with a group of people and could tell one guy might be trouble. He wasn't sporting a scar down one side of his face and looking to get in a fight—the kind of trouble he might bring was a bad vibe. He had made a point of asking if he could bring his guitar on the boat. I had no reason to object, but it sure didn't take much for him to whip out that guitar and start singing Jimmy Buffett songs, with his wife singing backup. And while I'm a fan of Jimmy Buffett, this guy wasn't doing Jimmy any favors— just had a lousy voice, and the presumption that came with it was that we were all supposed to love his singing and throw our underwear and hotel keys at him.

There were some other folks on the boat, and I could tell from the downcast eyes and hunched shoulders that they were not having a good time. But the performer sure was. So, the problem was: how could I get him to cork it without making him feel embarrassed? I needed a distraction. Luckily, I saw some dolphins in the back bay and brought them to everyone's attention, which was enough of an event to get him to put that guitar down. I just wanted to stay with those dolphins forever.

It was all something I had to file away in my memory bank for the next sail. I just had to know what worked and what didn't. Some people liked the action, and I learned to give them what they wanted.

And sometimes the action just found you all on its own.

We had the sails up, making great time for the Dry Tortugas, a couple of lines out the back snagging the occasional mackerel. Everyone was having a good time. But when everything is going right, with smiles on every face and rum in your belly, that's when you've got nowhere to go but down.

A good blow slammed into the sails, the impact making a *snap* on the canvas you could both hear and feel.

"It's really flying!" Josh said.

"Yeah, let's try to stay water-bound for now," I said.

The weather started to go south. Just started getting really snotty. I put the reef in the mainsail, pulled the jib in, lowered the sail on the mizzen mast, fired up the engine, and put it on autopilot. It wasn't a typhoon, and there was only maybe 20 feet of water below us, but anything deeper than about 6 feet and you could be treading water in it.

All of the sudden, the autopilot just went crazy, and the steering was all over the place. I went to the aft helm station to see if I could correct it, trying to figure out if it was the autopilot going on the fritz or if it was working fine but the steering was shot to hell. I took the wheel, the steering completely unresponsive.

"What's going on?" Josh asked.

"I think the steering cable snapped."

"Is that bad?"

"On a boat, you don't want anything to snap. But we can handle it."

I was lucky that *Rickshaw* actually had a redundant steering system. In addition to the main helm station aft, there was a separate steering station in the pilothouse. I explained that to Josh.

"So, we can just steer from there until we get to the Dry Tortugas? And then back home?"

"We could. But then if something goes wrong with the steering along the way, and we haven't made the repair already, then we're really"—I took a moment to search for the right word with more than four letters—"screwed."

"What's the difference?" he asked.

It was mostly about stability. With the steering functional at the pilothouse, that meant that we could keep our heading and our speed, and I could try to see what kind of fix I could make as we went in a mostly straight line at a mostly constant speed. But if that auxiliary steering went to pieces, then that meant that I'd have to try to repair both steering stations while the boat would be bobbing like a cork in a washing machine. Fixing something in a storm was bad, but fixing something inside of a boat that swayed like a drunk was impossible. I explained as much to Josh.

Rick took the wheel in the pilothouse. We had a quick discussion to diagnose the problem, and we were on the same page: the steering cable had probably snapped, and someone would need to go to the engine room and make sure the cable didn't get wrapped around something important, like the motor.

Now was when we played a fun game called "Not My Boat." The engine room was a shitty place to be, even in port, so making a repair there was a bit of a hardship duty.

"I guess this is really a job for the owner of the boat," I said.

"I'm not so sure," Rick said. "Isn't that the captain's job?"

"Aren't you at the wheel?"

"I'm just the helmsman. You're the one who's been making all the improvements to the boat."

"Right. So, I should be rewarded for that by taking the wheel while you go below."

"I probably wouldn't even be able to find my way with all the changes you've made," Rick said.

"You're clever. I trust you."

"How many beers have you had?"

"Maybe three."

"I've had fifty, so I should sit this one out."

"We only have a couple of six-packs in the coolers."

"The fact that I can't do the math tells you how drunk I am."

"I'll go below."

"It's probably for the best," Rick said, smiling.

I doubted that I'd be able to actually fix the steering cable while we were rolling around in 8-footers. My main concern was to make sure that the cable didn't get wrapped around the rudderpost and lock it in one position. We already had one thing busted—I didn't want it to get even more busted, or to damage any other parts of the boat.

When people hear "engine room," they might think of a scene in *Star Trek*, where Scotty is standing in an immense space with dozens of staff, trying to think of a way to make the engines go faster. But on *Rickshaw*, it was nothing like that. It was a tiny compartment, with barely enough room for me and a five-cell flashlight. I crawled behind the engine, through the bilges, trying to navigate the pitch-black conditions with the flashlight clamped between my chin and my shoulder so I could use my hands, trying to get hold of the broken cable.

Lots of people link "dark" with "cold," because winter is both of those things, but the engine room didn't offer that combo. Our diesel was going so we could maintain our direction, and that place was *hot*. It had to be over 160 degrees in there, and at the same time the engine was putting out temperature, it was also putting out noise. Hot as hell, dark as hell, loud as hell, smelled bad, and I didn't have any earphones for protection from the racket. I was digging around there, trying to find the cable, and of course it was wrapped up in a bunch of shit, so then I was trying to thread it back so it wouldn't gum up the works, sweating bullets while trying to avoid getting my arms caught in the motor. The burning oil and diesel smell didn't go very well with the three beers in my stomach, and I realized that it wasn't as fun as it had been just a few minutes before.

The motor was making the air hot as the Sahara, but it was a hell of a lot hotter on the surface of the motor itself. I tried to avoid it, but every now and then I'd lose balance or forget where it was, and I'd burn an arm or a leg pretty good. At least the pain helped keep my mind off my nausea. I still got seasick every time I went out, and the smell of the engine room wasn't doing me any favors. Added to that was the very idea of puking all over the place was making me feel even more sick, imagining that puke smell, which would only be improved by being sprayed over a hot engine room. I fought it back, because I didn't want to lose my lunch and, more than that, I didn't want the other guys to have to smell that kind of disgusting mess for the next three days.

I decided not to try to fix it completely. I just didn't want to risk losing or damaging the cable clamps I'd need for a repair. After forty-five minutes of sweating, swearing, and gagging, I managed to pull the cable back through the pulleys and steering gears so it would be ready for me when we got out of the bad weather.

I emerged from the engine room, glad to see Rick wasn't having any trouble steering from the pilothouse. If we lost steering there, then we'd have to take shifts hand steering it until we fixed it or got to a port. Standing in the evening air, I could really feel the temperature. It was still about 70 degrees, which wasn't cold, but it was about 100 degrees less than what I'd felt in the engine room. It was like walking into a refrigerator, and I wasn't feeling too good.

"Did you fix it?" Josh asked.

"I made sure the cable wasn't snagging on anything," I said.

"Does this mean we need to turn back?" he asked.

It was a fair question. While we had backup steering, there was a chance that the same thing that crippled the steering cable could happen again, and then we'd be in a bad place, especially if the weather stayed shitty. But that's not what I was thinking. I was thinking that we could do anything. We were a bunch of guys on a guys' weekend, and we felt strong, capable, and invincible. And a little buzzed. Maybe it would have been the smart thing to go back to Fort Myers and fix it in port, but that didn't even enter my brain as an option. We were tough hombres—nothing was going to make us turn tail and run. Besides that, we were past the point of no return. Basically, it's when you've crossed over the halfway point, where it's farther to turn back than it is to continue to your destination.

"No, we're going to stick to the plan," I said. "But can you do me a favor? Can you grab me some ice water from the cooler?"

I'd been down extracting the steering cable for about forty-five minutes, and I'd probably lost about five pounds in that heat. I wiped some of the grease off my hands while Josh brought me a plastic McDonald's cup full of water, and I just pounded it down. I drank it so fast that I didn't even taste it until it was gone.

Then I tasted fish. And realized that the water was a little thicker than water was usually supposed to be.

"Jesus, Josh, where the hell'd you get this?" I asked him.

"From the cooler."

"Which cooler?"

He pointed to one of the coolers that we had on board. But instead of the one we used to hold food and drinks, he pointed to the one we used to hold some of the mackerel that we'd already caught. Just a few fish that had spent the past eight hours rubbing their dead scales against the ice, which slowed, but did not stop, the growth of bacteria associated with dead tissue. I don't know if it was the thought of what I'd just drank, or my body trying to reject some absolute foulness, but about fifteen seconds later, that water made a U-turn, with me leaning over the side to feed the fish.

Just like old times.

Even though I knew, from my first moment working as a deckhand in Turks and Caicos, that I loved the sea, I also knew that it didn't love me nearly as much. I embraced the wide-open spaces and the wildlife and the smell of the salt air and the knowledge that I was doing something most people were incapable of doing, but the motion really got to me. For the first year of working on boats, I got pretty violently seasick. Every day, I'd hope it would be the day that my body would finally adjust to it, and every day, for about a year, I'd be disappointed. Much to the discomfort of those who had to witness that firsthand. Most people got accustomed to the rolling of the waves, though some never did. I knew one guy who worked at the waterfront that would get seasick just walking out on the dock. He'd had the same business for years, and he still couldn't walk onto a wooden dock without just about tossing his cookies. After about a year, I'd managed to put the worst of that seasickness behind me.

Unfortunately, I didn't usually have to contend with ingesting a pint of thick dead-fish juice. It had a way of unsettling the stomach. I was puking all the way to the Dry Tortugas. I tried to man my watch at the wheel, but it was just torture, hurling every couple of minutes, until I ran out of everything, and then dry heaving into a bucket. I called Rick over to help me, hoping he'd take pity on my unquestionably pitiful condition. But after a few minutes of my puking, he'd had his fill.

"I'm out of here," he said, moving to the ladder out of the pilothouse.

"Rick, I'm dying here, man." Not only was I sick, but I was dehydrated as hell. Everything was going out of me, and even the sight of a cup of water made me want to wretch, so nothing was coming in to fill the void. So, I was sick, tired, and running on empty.

"Tough shit, asshole."

He just walked off, leaving me, the bucket, and the boat.

After a few more hours of puking into that bucket, the only distraction being to look toward an inky-black horizon, I was overcome with relief when the sun started inching its way into the sky. There's something about the sun coming up after a night of storm-tossed seas that will bring a smile across even a dead man's face. I wasn't dead, but I had sure wished I was at times. Seven hours of blowing chunks was enough to give a man a strong case of fatigue and an equally large dose of self-pity.

I found a good place to drop the hook, killed the engine, and then had the pleasure of seeing the rest of the guys greeting the day by diving into some sandwiches and washing them down with a beer (except for Josh), and I was just dying. No beer, no food, no nothing for me, please. I just wanted to lie down and hopefully die.

After resting my head a bit, and getting some more time between us and the storm the day before, I decided that if I was going to be miserable, I might as well be miserable and useful. The steering cable still needed to be spliced together, and me feeling lousy wasn't going to get it done. Time to suck it up, cream puff. I gritted my teeth and went down below. The small flashlight wedged back under my chin, I fed the cable through the pulleys and steering gear, then I spliced the broken part of the cable to the part connected to the steering by attaching a pair of cable clamps. It was a bit of a tricky operation, because if it was too tight, then it was just going to snap again, and if it was too loose, there'd be too much play in the cable, making it possible for it to just pop off again like a loose bicycle chain.

Holding both ends of the cable, *and* both clamps, *and* a flashlight, it was enough to make me wish I was born with four hands instead of two. Finally, I had the cable threaded through the steering system with enough overlap that I was pretty confident it would hold, and then I attached the clamps. They didn't pop off immediately, which was always a good sign. I wasn't really an expert at repairing the steering system, but hell, a good sailor never learned anything in calm seas or tied to the dock.

"How's it look down there?" Rick asked when I emerged from the engine room. Like he really gave a shit.

"It's looking like it's held together with duck tape and bailing wire. How're things looking up here?" I asked.

"A little thin," he said.

"What are we running out of? We've only been gone a day. Fuel? Food?"

"Worse. Cigarettes," he said. Drunken sailors have a tendency to smoke more than usual, and they had blown through more than expected and we still had two days to go.

I was sweating like a whore in church, stomach felt like someone dropped a bowling ball on it from ten stories up, and he was worried about cigarettes.

Rick and Little Bobby must have felt pretty tense as I was unfouling the steering cable the night before, or while we were on the hook, because they had managed to burn through four days' worth of smokes in twenty-four hours. Now, a sailor can live without tobacco. But why would he want to?

The British Navy used to administer a ration of grog (water mixed with rum) to the sailors on board, and it wasn't to ensure that they performed their duties with greater skill and efficiency. They did it to give them a little buzz so they wouldn't kill all the officers and take Her Majesty's frigate to Tahiti. Remember the *Bounty*. You didn't want to deprive a man of his addictions mid-sail. The trouble was that there wasn't a convenience store for about 80 miles.

There's a great tradition at sea of the barter economy. In places that often lack supermarkets, gas stations, and department stores, often the only way to acquire items like fuel, food, and clothing is by trading what you've got in abundance. So, if you have a good haul of lobster or some extra foul-weather gear or some surplus fuel, that's something you can use to get the things you need.

And we needed cigarettes.

It may be a bad habit, but if you have smokers on board, and they run out of tobacco, they can become really difficult. Having four guys on a piece of real estate only 40 feet long means there's not a lot of room to just avoid someone who's snapping at everyone. It makes the trip a lot smoother just to find a carton of Marlboros.

After identifying what you need, the next step in the bartering process is identifying the best trading partner. One might think that because we were a sailboat, that we might more easily bond with the crew of another sailboat. But while sailboaters might have some good stories or useful tips on riding the waves, they just can't compare to the cornucopia of goods offered by powerboats.

Powerboats have everything. Usually, a big powerboat costs a lot more than a sailboat, and that means that the owner tends to have a lot of money. And while sailboats need to occupy a lot of space to accommodate sails and such, the powerboat just needs to have fuel. Powerboats were usually overflowing with everything you'd need when you're in need. So, we puttered right up to this big powerboat anchored just off Fort Jefferson and made our pitch.

"You guys have any extra smokes?" I asked.

"We might have a few packs lying around," the man from the powerboat replied. "You need to get rid of anything?"

"You need any rum?"

"Hell, we can never have enough rum."

Boats run on fuel and sailors run on rum.

Captain Morgan was our brand. I'd first discovered it on St. Thomas, and the guys and I just couldn't get enough. We raided all the liquor stores on the island, filling our hold with fourteen cases of the stuff. It wasn't something I was in a rush to part with, but sometimes, you just had to bite the bullet.

"How about any ice?" I asked.

"Yeah, we can make you some ice."

Of course they had ice. Probably had a Sub-Zero fridge that made ice by the ton and was fully stocked with rib-eye steaks and Dom Pérignon. Powerboaters really lived the life.

Our stores of cigarettes stocked high enough to prevent a mutiny, I moved on to our next order of business: checking out the birds.

There was an amazing bird sanctuary near Bush Key in the Dry Tortugas National Park. The place was a kind of perfect layover spot for birds migrating from one America to the other. There was just an amazing diversity of the birds you could see there: peregrine falcons (the fastest animal on earth, for anyone hoping to win a bar bet), ruby-throated hummingbirds, yellow-billed cuckoos, double-crested cormorants, and scores of others. Where it's warm and where there are fish, just incredible animals will appear.

This was another benefit of life on boats. When you could cross the waves, you could see things that most of the world never could. You had access to experiences that 99 percent of the rest of the world was denied. Being able to see those birds was like being able to see a flower that only grew on the top of Mount Everest.

Though, horribly, there were no fish. While we had an amazing time snorkeling there, we came up pitifully when we actually got out our gear and tried fishing. Just couldn't get anything to bite. Maybe all the fish were still full from all the chow I'd puked into the drink the day before and couldn't be bothered to go after our bait.

When we saw all there was to see, and were running low on rum and cigarettes, it was time to head home. But the same specter that scared away the fish scared the wind, too, and there was just nothing pushing us home. The water was so calm, so glassy, that you could have had a shave without getting a nick. We really could have used that wind, too, since it was in the nineties all day, and it would have been nice to get a little respite. We cranked up the diesel and set course for home.

Rickshaw wasn't outfitted with any kind of fancy electronic navigation, but we didn't need that crap. We were sailors. We were able to use dead reckoning and the charts. Hell, it was our own backyard—we could just sail by where we needed to go, like navigating hometown roads without ever having to look at a street sign.

Not the most productive fishing trip, but the thing about going to sea is that you never make a trip where the ocean doesn't teach you a life lesson, provided you survive it.

Chapter 6

What's the Difference Between God and a Captain? God Doesn't Think He's a Captain.

Starting out, you take the work you can get. There's no peaches and cream on day one. You've got to earn your spot. I wanted to be among the elite, and the only way to be elite at anything, whether it be as a starting quarterback or a Hollywood actor or a sailor, is to begin at the bottom. And at the bottom, some people could be cheap, some could be crazy, and if you were really lucky, you could get both.

Earl was a good guy, owned a nice 40-foot, single-engine, custom-built sport fish. It was a good little boat, though having just a single engine provided some problems for sport fishing. If you had a two-engine boat, then you could steer with the engines. Usually, you fish by trailing your bait and lines out the stern and hope you get a strike. If you just have one engine, then the only way to go after the fish was to put her in reverse, which would drain water into the cockpit and then back out the scuppers. But if you had two engines, you could take one of the engines out of gear and let the other engine steer the boat in reverse. But having two engines would have cost more money, and if there was one thing Earl was good at, it was finding a way not to spend money.

I'd heard about the job from an ad. Earl said he needed a captain, and I needed the hours. The more hours you work, the bigger the craft you can work. A 40-footer wasn't an enormous boat, so it was within my area of expertise. I just wasn't sure why he needed me in the first place.

"Out there, you're the captain," Earl said.

"All right," I said.

"But it's my boat, and I like to drive it," he added.

I thought to ask why he wanted to hire someone, at $100 a day, when he was planning on doing a lot of the work himself. And then I remembered that I liked money and wanted the job.

"You're the boss," I said. Hell, if he wanted to hire me to watch him steer the boat, shop for groceries, and make himself martinis, I'd allow that, too.

That's just how Earl liked things. He liked being in control. And, for the most part, it worked out fine. He hired me as the captain, another crewman as a mate, and we helped operate the boat when he'd go on fishing trips. Even if he did things differently than I would have.

We fished in the Gulf of Mexico. We'd take his boat out, fuel up in Key West, and then head to Isla Mujeres (the Island of Women), an island in the Caribbean about ten miles off the coast of Cancun. On one trip, Earl had three friends with him and everyone seemed to be having a good time.

"Not too bad out here," Earl said.

"It's gorgeous," I agreed.

"These guys are sure getting their money's worth," he said.

I chuckled. After all, this wasn't a charter, this was a boat full of Earl's buddies. But even though I thought it had to have been a joke, he wasn't laughing.

"You're serious? You're charging your friends for this trip?"

"Hey, just a little something to pay for the beer and gas," he replied.

That was Earl—one of the cheapest guys I ever met. Earl could squeeze a nickel until the buffalo shit. Who made their own friends pay for a fishing vacation? Earl had made his money from storage facilities he owned, but being good with dollars and cents didn't make him good with common sense.

His friends weren't the only ones who had to suffer because of his cheapness. He was the kind of guy who wouldn't drive out of a parking space if there was still time left on the meter. He'd rather waste fifteen minutes sitting in that parked car if it meant that he'd get what he paid for. His tightness with the dollar almost stranded us in the middle of the ocean.

We'd been motoring down south, when all of the sudden, the engine (an 892 Detroit) died. Then the generator died. Was it because we'd ventured into the Bermuda Triangle, where the rules of time and space ceased to function? No, it was because Earl wouldn't replace the $12 fuel filters until they were so clogged with gunk that they'd trigger an automatic shutdown. And this wasn't something that, by any means, had to happen. Earl knew from the moment we started the engines that the pressure on the fuel gauges was in the red. But, to his mind, why change them in port, just because they were redlining? The only way to know for sure if he'd gotten full use out of those filters was if he pushed them past the point of failure. Then he'd know that he'd gotten his money's worth.

The problem was, that's a pretty dangerous way to live your life. If you start the engines in port and see that the fuel filters are almost completely blocked, then you can kill power, change the filters, and restart. Now, if you *still* have a problem, like if the new filters are defective, or if there's some other problem that's causing the redlining, then you have all the resources of the port to fix it. But if it happens out in the middle of nowhere? Then you are, potentially, screwed, drifting aimlessly miles away from civilization with no way to get back save for getting out and pushing. And for what? To ensure another two hours of life on a $12 filter?

"Filter's gone," Earl said.

"Yep," I replied. "You saw that it was redlining on the pressure gauges since we left the dock."

"You want to change it?"

"I wanted to change the filters before we left. You're the one said we had to keep it going. Why don't you change the filters?"

When our engine died, we were between Cuba and the Yucatán Peninsula. That was a little too close to Castro's backyard for my comfort. A couple of friendly Cuban sailors come up on us, and the next thing you know, our boat is part of Fidel's fishing fleet. No thank you.

Earl could tell I was in no mood to screw around, so he changed his own filters.

And it wasn't just the cheapness. Or maybe it would be more accurate to say that the cheapness was part of some bigger problem with Earl, part of a pattern where the most seemingly insignificant things would set him off. He just had a sensitivity for stuff that wouldn't even register for most people. The man had a temper.

One day, we were doing our usual, fishing for sailfish, which are similar to swordfish, and can look really nice above your mantel, clocking in at about 10 feet long and maybe 200 pounds. But the thing is, the sailfish didn't like to come out early in the day. In the early morning, the only fish in the water were bonito, or boneheads as we'd call them. Now, bonito are a perfectly good fish and taste kind of like skipjack tuna. But we'd come for sailfish, and maybe some mahi-mahi, and not bonito.

And that would have been fine if we just fished for the sailfish when we knew that they'd be out biting, around ten in the morning or later. They wouldn't come out until the boneheads left. But Earl, he had it in his mind that the early bird gets the worm, so he wanted to start fishing for them just after the sun came up, at about seven in the morning. In his mind, time was money, and waiting around until ten was just wasting both. So, we got our hooks out, and we were getting a lot of boneheads. And it was just driving Earl crazy. After pulling up his sixth bonehead, Earl just lost it and took out his knife and hacked that thing to pieces, right in front of everyone. I was on the fly bridge, looking down on him as he did it, and it was pretty horrible to behold. The bonehead weighed in at 10 to 12 pounds, and Earl just attacked it like Jack the Ripper, hacking it maybe fifteen times until there wasn't anything left of it but a handful of gristle and a boat covered in blood.

He's sharp, I said to myself. Reminds me of an old joke: what's the difference between God and a captain? God doesn't think he's a captain. And Earl may have just been an owner, but the way he was hacking at that fish, you had to wonder if he thought he was Poseidon himself.

It wasn't like that one fish was the reason we weren't catching any sailfish. And it wasn't personal, like that fish had set out to ruin Earl's day. It wasn't even a big deal! All we had to do was wait a few hours until the boneheads were gone, and we'd start catching the sailfish. But that just wasn't acceptable for Earl, who seemed to think that every hour we waited was some kind of personal loss he could never get back. The man just didn't understand how to optimize his time.

This isn't to say it was all bad. One of the most amazing experiences of my life happened while I was working on Earl's boat near Isla Mujeres. I was able to witness an event called a green flash. Sometimes, when the atmospheric conditions are perfect, and the sun goes down below the horizon, you'll see a bright explosion of green light. It only lasts for a second or two, and is so rare, that some people think it's a myth, but it's an actual optical phenomenon that has been witnessed and recorded and happens when the atmosphere causes the sun's light to separate out into different colors.

I was right there on Earl's boat when it happened, standing next to the mate looking out toward the horizon to watch the sun set. And then it was like an enormous firework erupted, splashing the world in green. Both the mate and I saw it, though at first we couldn't believe it. It happened that day, it happened the next day, and I've never seen it since, though I'm grateful to have been able to see it at all.

It was beautiful, but it didn't last very long, and that's a pretty good way to sum up my time working with Earl. We had a good run, and I worked with him doing fishing trips for about a year, but then we ran into an explosion of cheapness and ego.

We had just come back from a monthlong fishing trip. For a variety of reasons, the trip ended a bit earlier than trips like that usually do, at about noon. We were cleaning things up and squaring things away on the boat, and I was mentally preparing to go home and get a little rest. That's when Earl came up to me and made his wishes known.

He looked at his watch, then looked at me, kind of shrugged, and said, "You can finish out the day by doing some yardwork."

"Excuse me?" I asked. I was paid $100 a day, but I wasn't the one who decided to pack it in at noon. If Earl and his buddies wanted to call it a day and have lunch at the pier, that was their business, but my day was done.

"I'm paying you by the day. A standard day is eight hours. We've only been working for four hours. If you want to get paid in full, then come over to my house and pull some weeds and rip out some stumps."

"Earl, I'm a captain. I'm an expert at operating a boat, and that's what you're paying me for. You want a landscaper, you hire a landscaper."

"That ain't right. I pay you for the day, I expect a day's work."

"You think the barber gives discounts for guys going bald? A haircut's a haircut. And when you tie this boat to the pier, the haircut's over. Pay the barber."

"I expect a full day of work."

"You want to do some more fishing, we can do that. You want a spin around the harbor, that's fine. But I'm not going to cut your grass or wash your truck or do your laundry or paint your damn house. I'm a captain, and you pay me to do a captain's job. You want a foot massage, that's not the business I'm in."

"If you're not going to work, then I don't have to pay you."

"Fine. You pay me for what I've done, and I'm out of here."

A month of sailing with the guy, and we stop working together because he insisted on giving me $3,050 instead of $3,100. But you don't get to stick your tongue down a girl's throat just because you bought her a drink at the bar, and I don't have to wash your damn windows just because you hired me to captain your boat.

There was other work out there.

The work wasn't always glamorous. When you're trying to get every job you can to get more hours, to get more experience, to get more money, those jobs will never be glamorous. Those jobs were work. A means to an end. If you want to be captain of a mega-yacht eventually, and the only job you will take is the captain of a mega-yacht, then you'll never be captain of anything. You've got to pay your dues.

Part of that meant a lot of day sails, working on these 70-foot head boats, with forty-five to fifty tourists fishing cheek-to-jowl. I'd hand every man, woman, and child a fishing rod, and once we started to drift, I'd spend the rest of the day cutting bait for chum and baiting people's rods, and then taking fish off the hook and cleaning what they caught. It was a bit monotonous, but at the same time, I was out on the water on a nice day, catching fish, and what's not to like? It wasn't particularly challenging as a feat of seamanship, or as a feat of angling, but it was a job. It was mostly working for tips, and it paid enough to get me to the next job.

Sometimes, things sounded a bit more alluring than they turned out to be. For a time, I did work on a casino boat. At that point, I had a captain's license, but I was only hired as the first officer. To increase the size of my license, I had to work bigger boats. When lots of people hear "casino," they get visions of James Bond or *Ocean's Eleven* and imagine that it's all tuxedos and beautiful people and international intrigue, but the reality is something significantly less glamorous.

These were 200-foot boats, converted mud boats from oil rigs, that carried a crew of twelve. It was a geographical and financial cruise to nowhere.

Our mission was to load up the boat with as many gamers as we could possibly carry, then head out into international waters, where it was no longer illegal to gamble. So, if you were in a city that didn't permit games of chance, you'd just have to go nine miles out to be beyond the boundary of state legal jurisdictions. That's in the Gulf of Mexico. On the Atlantic side, it's only three miles. Not sure why. Once past that line, the fun began.

Though it wasn't actually that exciting, from a sailor's perspective. There's nothing difficult about heading out to sea, reaching the nine-mile limit, and then doing long, lazy circles for four hours. You just try to keep the boat comfortable and let the players have their fun.

And there was fun to be had. The boat had multiple decks, and in addition to craps, blackjack, roulette, and slot machines, there was a restaurant (good but not great—about the same quality as a Golden Corral, with prime rib thinner than the soles of my shoes) and a theater where the non-gamers could catch a live band or a stand-up comic or vaudeville act or a magic act. The good news was the show was included in the $40 price of admission. The bad news was that the crème de la crème of entertainers don't gravitate toward working casinos (water-based or otherwise). The people who were on that boat were there to gamble, and the only reason they'd be visiting the theater was because they'd busted, they'd come as the date for someone who was still on the gaming floor, or they needed someplace to try to recover from motion sickness. It was not the most receptive crowd for warmed-over jokes about airline peanuts or ventriloquists getting into arguments with their puppets. The entertainment was basically a way for people who had lost $500 at the tables to convince themselves that they were getting their money's worth.

Some people think that such excursions might risk the threat of a bad element, the temptation for thieves or heist artists to try to make a quick score. But being on a boat really cuts into the incentive for any kind of crazy action. There was security all over the ship, dozens of uniformed guards in addition to tons of video cameras, and if someone wanted to try to steal from a player, where were they going to run to? They couldn't just grab a rack of chips and race out the front door. They couldn't raid the counting room and catch a taxi to the airport. No, high-stakes thievery wasn't something that plagued the casino ships. The biggest threat was seasickness.

The general rule for the captain of a casino ship was: take your time so you can make some money. The odds always favored the house, and with nowhere to really go, the players were forced to grapple with the pure statistics of most casino games until they'd bust. No casino boat was built off the backs of winning players. As a captain, the safety of your passengers and crew is paramount, but at the same time, there's a lot of incentive to stay out as long as possible. For a lot of casino boats, the captain is paid a flat salary plus some percentage of the profits for the night. So even if it's a gale-force hurricane, a captain's going to want to stay out as long as possible.

Inevitably, people got sick. The ship could carry about four hundred people comfortably, but once we left the dock, a lot of them started feeling pretty uncomfortable. There were times when half the passengers would be throwing up. I'd hand out pillows and blankets to people, watch them curl up miserable in a corner and try not to think about the waves.

Part of the reason that passengers felt so lousy was because the boat itself wasn't the best vessel for the job. The owners who bought it wanted something cheap that could carry a lot of people, and they outfitted the interior nicely, but it was old, it didn't ride well, and it belched smoke all over the place. Designed to carry mud for the oil rigs, it had a flat bottom with a shallow draft that didn't take waves particularly well. It didn't have stabilizers, so it would rock and roll from one side to the other pretty easily. Nobody thought to upgrade the ride, because it was the kind of business where you didn't make money by spending money. It wasn't unsafe, but it wasn't a pleasure cruise. No one was taking pictures of the boat so they could proudly declare, "Look what I went out on, Mom!" I thought it was hilarious, but few people shared my sick sense of humor.

One of the enduring images I had of working those casino boats was one woman so obsessed with the one-arm bandits, the slot machines, that, despite the fact that the motion of the ship was clearly making her nauseated, she just wouldn't give up. She had a couple of coin buckets with her, like a lot of the veteran players tended to do, with one earmarked for coins that would go into the machine, and another, empty bucket, to catch all the winnings she was anticipating. One arm cradled around the bucket of change, the other, slightly more developed and muscular arm, pulling down the lever. But this woman added a third bucket—for puking into. She was so sick that she kept retching, but she was so *determined* that she wouldn't go lie down. Quarter in, pull the lever, puke, wipe mouth, quarter in, pull the lever, etc.

We eventually had to intercede. In part, this was because she was clearly having a rough time with motion sickness and needed a break. But it was also because it was pretty disruptive to the rest of the guests, this woman holding a bucket of sick and waving it around. It created a perimeter of empty machines around her, and part of our job was to ensure that there were as few unmanned slot machines on board as possible. We finally had a word with her about taking a break, but she didn't go quietly into that good night. She put up a bit of a stink before finally agreeing to lie down. After a pretty short interval, she'd sneak away and be right at it again.

On the one hand, it seemed a little sad, that she was clearly miserable from seasickness and still unwilling to call it quits. On the other hand, she must have gotten some thrill out of it, a thrill that was at least a little greater than the misery of her body, because she kept plugging away. Do what you love, and you'll never work a day in your life, I suppose. It certainly wasn't the captain's job to legislate morality. And, looking at it dispassionately, this was a casino cruise. Gambling was specifically what most of them had

Having a cold one after making landfall in St. Bart's during my early career.

Mary Anne and me at Capt. Tony's Saloon in Key West.

Headed out for a day sail in Fort Myers Beach. Building the sea time.

On our way to the Dry Tortugas aboard *Rickshaw* before the steering cable snapped and I got some of the worst food poisoning known to man, courtesy of accidentally drinking the water this fish was being kept in.

Sunset over the Gulf of Mexico on our way to Key West.

One of my earliest commands, *Rickshaw*. Lots of blood, sweat, and tears went into her (Fort Myers Beach).

Some live music at our place in Turks and Caicos, the Columbus Club. That's how we rolled down on the island.

No idea what I was thinking inside the Columbus Club, but it looks important (Turks and Caicos).

Our bar in the Turtle Cove restaurant. The bar was literally a boat sawed in half. That should have told me something right then . . .

My son's eleventh birthday, and his first time on the ocean on the sport fish named *Sandbox* (Turks and Caicos).

Getting sea time on *Mombo,* sport fish style. Going from Turks and Caicos back to the States.

Best first mate I've ever had, my wife, Mary Anne, on board *Rickshaw*.

Night watch on *Rickshaw*. Gotta be vigilant (Fort Myers Beach).

This is how you celebrate Christmas at sea: helm station cluttered with decorations courtesy of Mary Anne (Fort Myers Beach).

At the helm of *Southern Nights* on our way to Nassau. I didn't realize until after the Coast Guard boarded us that it was a drug boat.

In the cockpit of *Mombo,* the sport fish I cut my teeth on with Captain Rick.

Captain Rick and me getting ready for the St. Thomas Boy Scout Invitational sport fishing tournament. This was right after almost getting killed delivering a boat to the British Virgin Islands with an eccentric character named Crazy George.

Interior shot of our open-air restaurant over the water in Turtle Cove, Turks and Caicos.

Always on the lookout on *Rickshaw* (Key West).

It's always nice when the rainbow appears. The worst is over. On our way to the Bahamas on *Rickshaw*.

Taking a break from day sailing on *Rickshaw*, nothing better. Sails up, autopilot on, and someone else doing lookout.

Me manning the DJ station before I got bit by the call of the sea (Turks and Caicos).

Our new restaurant in Turks and Caicos in 1986—lots of work to be done.

My son Josh and his friend on their surfboards under our restaurant in Turtle Cove (Turks and Caicos).

Checking the rigging during a blow in the Bahamas.

Weather isn't always pleasant on a small sailboat (Bahamas).

Stopped in Key West and had a Captain and Coke, my signature beverage, at the famous Capt. Tony's Saloon.

One of my very first solo trips on *Rickshaw* with Mary Anne, offshore of Little Palm Island, just before Key West.

come for in the first place, so who was I to say, "Lady, maybe gambling isn't in your best interests." On that boat, gambling was in everyone's best interests.

If you interrupted those diehards, you were taking your life into your own hands. I'd seen those veteran slot-pullers leave their seat for a quick bathroom break only to discover their machine—*their* machine—had been commandeered by some clueless interloper. He didn't understand that *that* particular slot machine was temporarily the private property of an eighty-year-old blue tip from Boca Raton. That newbie didn't realize that this woman had plugged $18 worth of quarters into that machine, and it was therefore on the verge of *paying out*. The money in that machine was *her* money. If that man didn't quit the premises and do so quick, he was in for a bigger hurt than any cat-o-nine-tails could dole out.

My job was in the wheelhouse, driving the boat. The captain would often oversee leaving the dock and bringing it back to the pier, but he'd rarely drive once we were under way. It was a voyage to nowhere, so there wasn't a ton of cutting-edge navigation and seamanship one would have to display. The biggest challenge at sea was making sure that we didn't run into a fishing boat or a shrimping boat, which were lit up like Christmas trees anyway, so we'd watch our radars and scopes and make sure we didn't plow through someone's gunwale.

It was reliable work, but I was looking for something more interesting. Dodging shrimp boats for six hours a day is like dying a slow, painful, agonizing death, one six-hour shift at a time. That, compounded with the fact that the captain and I didn't quite see eye-to-eye, made me think my future might be elsewhere.

He was a necessary evil, as far as I was concerned. He did his job, and I did mine, but we weren't Butch and Sundance. He needed me because I was dependable, I showed up on time, and I did my job well in an area where the labor pool was severely challenged. I needed him to hire me in the first place. But there were some personality problems between us, most notably that he was having an affair with the chief stewardess. Not smart as a boss, and not smart as a married man. And not something I approved of. But hey, I didn't have to like him, and we didn't hang out together—his business, not mine. But especially in a small town where everyone knew each other, taking a dump where you eat is probably not the brightest move you could make.

It was bad enough that he was doing it, but he made it worse by trying to pull me into his shit sandwich. His wife had suspicions, and it didn't take a genius for those suspicions to take root. Hell, when the boat's supposed to dock at midnight, and the captain doesn't come home until four in the morning smelling like the chief stew's perfume, you can't always try to blame it on paperwork and traffic. Eventually, he could see that wasn't working anymore, so he tried to get me to cover for him in front of his wife.

"Lee, do me a favor. When my wife comes on board, just tell her you were with me when we had to work late last week."

"Which day?"

"Every day."

"I don't think so," I said.

"What are you talking about?" he asked, angry.

"Hey, just because you've compromised your morals doesn't mean I have to compromise mine. Hell, you stand a better chance of seeing God twice than that happening. I'm not going to let the cat out of the bag, but I'm sure as hell not going to lie for you."

"You're really putting me in a tough position here."

"You put yourself there. If you don't want to worry about the lie, then don't do the deed. But if she asks when we pull into the dock, I'm going to tell her."

That's what put an end to my chances of becoming captain on that boat. The man in the chair wasn't going to recommend me, and I wasn't going to stick around getting bored out of my gourd with no future. Time to look for something new. I lost track of that guy the moment my feet left the gangplank.

We had decided to move to Fort Lauderdale, where there was more opportunity for me and my newfound career. Fort Lauderdale, the yachting capital of the world. That's where I found a great owner. Though, when looking for something interesting, you have to beware what you wish for.

There are lots of things that can make a great owner, but it's not really rocket science. Being a good owner is like being any kind of good boss. You pay your staff on time. You understand that you're paying for someone's time, you're not renting a person. You don't have to treat people like dogs in order for them to understand that you're an authority figure. You pay people for their skills and expertise, and don't second-guess them when they utilize those skills and expertise. If you possess those basic qualities, then you stand to make a good owner.

Pauly was a good owner. He was a real estate guy, a deal maker from Atlanta who owned a lot of property and a few bars and restaurants. He wasn't the kind of guy who would leave any stone unturned. Even when he owned a building and had every square foot of livable or workable space rented out or sold, he'd find ways to make a dollar or two on top of that. Literally, he would rent out space on his rooftops to cell towers. He owned a couple of private planes, and he made his home in Atlanta, where he lived in a huge mansion. Despite his money, he'd treat people like family.

This isn't to say that Pauly was a pushover. I worked hard when I was the captain of his boat, the *Pauly D*. No matter what model or size of boat he'd get, or what he'd upgrade to, it always remained the *Pauly D*. The man knew his brand, I suppose. That first boat was a 55-foot Sea Ray. Pretty well-built boat for what it was. I went into it with a bit of a negative bias against that particular model, since I'd seen a lot of Sea Rays cruising up and down the inter-coastal, throwing a wall of water that would just rock the hell out of anybody nearby. Those boats were typically owner operated, which meant idiots were out there driving big boats when they had no business doing it. I used to say, "I'd rather have a sister in a whore-house than a brother that owned a Sea Ray." It just seemed like kind of a douche magnet. But there I was—running one.

When Pauly first hired me, I was a bit worried that it was going to be a job with a very limited longevity. In those early days, he loved to party. When I started working for him on that Sea Ray (before he upgraded to a 65-foot Intermarine, a nice fast boat, pretty roomy, though not particularly attractive), I won-dered if I should be getting hazard pay. Pauly was just the kind of guy who didn't spend a lot of time idling in neutral.

Pauly really liked to get a head start on the weekend. He'd come in on a Thursday—that was ladies' night. He'd pick up some friends, sometimes up to forty people, which included more than a few beautiful women, and he'd be up until four in the morning, traveling from Fort Lauderdale to their docks. He'd bring on a bunch of his friends, then motor over to the Diplomat Hotel, dock the boat, and invite a ton of people from the hotel over to come join the party. Once, he'd brought in so many people that the boat literally started listing to one side at the dock. I had to kick some people off, just so the boat would level out. That would be a tough one to put on the résumé—being the captain of a boat that sunk while tied to the dock!

Then we'd go out for a cruise, and it would be a challenge. The music would be blaring, there'd be tons of people milling around, and parties were something that worked better at night, so I'd be driving blind, moving around in pitch black, running the boat entirely by instruments, just trying to get everyone from point A to point B safely.

On more than one occasion, I'd be there with Pauly, watching the sun come up. Four hours later, he'd have some rest while I took the boat back to our docks in Lauderdale, and then he'd be raring to do it all over again. So, we'd head down to Miami Beach and party on South Beach until the wee small hours of the morning. Pauly would head to his cabin to recharge, and I'd take the boat back to our dock. Saturday night, we'd head over to Riverwalk, have some fun. Sunday was a recovery day. We'd just take a nice easy cruise, since everyone was pretty spent from burning the candle at both ends.

Come Monday, Pauly would jump on his jet and head back to Atlanta. You might think that this would be my time to finally recover a bit myself. That would be my weekend, right? But there just wasn't any time, because I only had basically Tuesday and Wednesday to get the boat cleaned up and our stores replenished before Pauly came back down on Thursday to start it up again. Week after week, like clockwork! For months on end. Finally, after about three months of this, of nonstop partying followed by nonstop prep followed by more partying, I had to have a come-to-Jesus talk.

"Pauly, I have to talk to you about something."

"What's up?"

"We can't keep running this hard. We go like madmen for four days straight, then I take two days to clean and fix everything that gets pulled apart, then we start it all over again."

"But everyone seems to be having a good time," he said.

"No one's saying they're not. But the crew just can't take it. You're burning them out. Pretty soon, we're going to start losing people. Good people. They'll sign on somewhere else for better hours and the same pay."

"So, what do you think I should do? Pay them more?"

"It's not about the money. But it's like lifting. You can't move a quarter ton of iron every day and do the same thing the next day. You need to put a rest day in there. And the same goes for the crew. We can do this, but it needs to be every other week, at the most."

"It's my boat."

"And I'm just trying to tell you how to make your boat work the best way."

He agreed. He didn't fire me or tell me, "My way or the highway." He knew I wasn't soft, knew I wasn't asking him just to make a power play. He treated me like a professional, and we scaled things back.

This isn't to say that he couldn't fly off the handle every now and then.

Once, we were in the middle of one of our recovery cycles. Me and the stew were loading up supplies, and Pauly arrived early and wanted to take a shower on the boat. But we hadn't finished replenishing our stores, and one of the things we were low on was fresh water for the showers and the taps. We were close to being dry as a bone, which was one of the reasons we'd brought the party to a close.

He rang me up on my cell. "Lee, I'm in the middle of my shower, but there's no more water!"

"Relax, Pauly. Nothing's broken. We just need to refill the water tanks. I'll be back to the docks in five minutes and get everything squared away. Just relax."

Relaxing just wasn't the way Pauly liked to have fun. He had to be in constant motion, even if he wasn't entirely sure what he was doing.

Filling up the boat's water supplies wasn't a complicated operation. You just had to go to the dock, grab the hose, stick it in the fill tank, and fill it up. But since Pauly had showed up early, and unannounced, I had no idea that I'd need to have the boat ready for him. He didn't want to wait for me to finish the supply run and figured that he'd be able to fill those water tanks by himself. He was right that he knew where the hose was to the fresh water, and he knew the water tanks were in the back of the boat. But he wasn't quite so on-the-mark about where to fill it. He found an opening about the right size for a hose, opened it up, the hose fit in pretty well, and he started filling it. But the thing is, there's lots of things that go into a boat using a hose.

And one of them is fuel.

He stuck the hose in and filled the not-quite-empty fuel tanks full of water.

Not a good move.

The boat wasn't made with some kind of automatic shutoff when water gets pumped into the fuel tanks. So, when he started pumping, the water just filled up and eventually overflowed.

When I came back, I knew immediately that something was wrong.

"What's that fuel smell?" I asked the stew. She shook her head. It didn't take long to find the answer.

There was fuel all over the decks, just a huge mess. I found Pauly pretty quick, and we diagnosed the problem in two seconds.

"When can we head out?" he asked.

"Pauly, this boat ain't going anywhere. I got to get the deck cleaned up, I got to pump out all the fuel tanks and get them polished. Then we have to get it refueled."

"How long's that going to take? An hour?"

"Pauly, your lack of patience just killed the entire weekend. Don't stay here. Get a hotel room in town. It's going to take a while to clean up this mess."

Pauly had fucked up. But he knew that he had fucked up. The lost fuel and the cleanup ended up costing him about $8,000. And that's not $8,000 he was spending on a nice watch or a couple of slick suits or a first-class flight to Rome. This was an $8,000 fuckup that didn't buy any fun.

But the thing was, he didn't fly off the handle. He didn't blame me for not anticipating that he'd arrive early or blow his stack that I hadn't taught him how to fill up the water tanks properly. He didn't fire me because he'd cost himself 8K on my watch. He knew he'd screwed up, he didn't blame anybody else, and he moved on. It was a bitter pill to swallow, but he was a stand-up guy. Sure, he made some extra work for all of us, but that's the nature of the beast. Everyone makes mistakes, but very few will own them. Got to give credit where it's due.

Later, Pauly added a 90-foot Johnson to his fleet. Guys who buy yachts only move up in size. They almost never make a lateral move or downsize. If they're going to make a change, it's going to be bigger. We had the boat shipped over to California. I had to go out and pick it up, then we had to break it in after we had it shipped to Florida from Ensenada, Mexico. People think that getting something new is the best way to get something, but there's a lot of advantage in acquiring something used. If a boat, or a house, or anything of value, has been used for a few years, you know it's not going to crap out on you. If you get something new, there's a host of problems that could come up right out of the gate. For a boat, you have to break in the engine, you have to make sure you don't have any leaks, you have to check that all the electrical components work, all the plumbing works. Hell, you have to make sure the humidity doesn't make wooden doors swell so they don't close right. Lots can go wrong during that break-in period.

And it did.

The manufacturer had installed the wrong-sized O-rings on the oil plugs for the mains. The O-rings are pretty small, but on a boat that size, for the amount of money it cost, it was an important little detail. We were coming back from Key West, and it just blew the O-ring out, the thing just went, and we lost all the oil in the port main with the starboard one probably right behind it. The engine room was just covered in oil. The engine room, which had been brand new, pristine, spotless, so clean they should have offered it as a color at True Value, New Engine Room White, was just coated in black, nasty-ass diesel oil from top to bottom.

When something like that happens on a boat, you don't just say, "Shit, something's wrong, let's hope it works itself out." As soon as we lost the port main, the computers shut down the engine in under a second. Alarms started blaring, making it sound like World War III had been declared. I saw that the port engine was dead, so I went to the engine room to get an assessment, saw the whole area was totally wasted. Each main took 55 gallons of oil. Imagine 55 gallons of oil exploding in a 20-by-20-foot room.

I knew how much oil had escaped the portside main, so the first thing I did was shut down our bilges so we didn't pump all the oil overboard. Then I had to satisfy the Coast Guard that we didn't create an ecological disaster.

The Coast Guard is pretty concerned about any potential oil spills around the Keys. Damage those reefs, and they'll put you so far away, they'll have to pipe sunshine to your ass. And even though it's never a picnic when you have to call the Coast Guard, things go a lot smoother when you call as soon as a problem happens, rather than wait for them to find you. Then they're in a bad mood, and you're the reason for it.

There's a lot you have to ascertain. What killed our engine? We had to make sure we didn't hit anything, didn't have any hull breaches, weren't taking on any water, that we weren't pumping any oil out, that everything was good on the starboard engine. Then I had to give the bad news to the owner.

"Pauly, we may have just puked the main."

"Shit," he said. It was just one word, but it was entirely on the money. Those mains were about 250K a piece. And that's plucking one off the factory floor. Doesn't count parts, labor, and installation. And installation of those things was a bitch. You had to cut a hole into the side of the ship just to get one of those in there. Then you had to patch the hole, which meant ripping out all the piping, all the plumbing, all the electrical, and then putting it all back in there. Even if the manufacturer was going to have to eat that cost for their fuckup, it was going to be a hefty bill, and it was going to require a hell of a lot of work to un-fuck.

One main was down, though the generators were still running, so we had A/C and lights. The port engine was just dead, so we had to try to make way on the starboard engine, getting us maybe 7 or 8 knots. You couldn't even go into the engine room, with all the oil still dripping down from the ceiling.

"How long will it take to get back?" Pauly asked.

"At this speed? You might want to get a sandwich from the galley, since it's going to be a while."

"But it doesn't have to."

Pauly, like most of us, didn't want to hang around while we limped into port for repairs. But, unlike most of us, he has a big checkbook and a lot of pull. I called a friend to come pick him and his guests up, and he got to zip out of there and back home.

That left me alone with the crew, going upriver on one main, which wasn't easy. The river was very narrow, with a lot of intricate passageways, the kind of place you really want to have all your power and maneuverability. Anything over a hundred feet I'd prefer to get towed up with tugs. Under a hundred, I'd drive it myself. It wasn't as though you couldn't drive the larger yachts up the river, it was out of concern for the recreational boaters if they didn't have their radios on, or weren't paying attention, they'd miss the fact that you were bringing a monster up the river and they had better stay clear. With tugs, they have more control over your boat and they also assume responsibility for it. If I screw up, the owner pays; if the tugs make a mistake, they pay. On big boats, it just makes sense to have that cheap insurance against the what-ifs. At any rate we made it in, eventually.

We arrived late, about nine hours after we'd been expected. It was pitch black, and I had to dock the boat with just one engine and a bow thruster, and there were a lot of moving parts with that operation, but we managed to put her where she needed to go.

It took about three months in the yard to get everything cleaned and fixed. They actually tried to blame the engine failure on me. When the manufacturer's rep showed up, he went right to the starboard engine and pulled the dipstick out. He looked at it and then over to me and said, "Were both mains carrying the same amount of oil?" I said sure, within a couple of quarts I suppose. He then asked me why I would overfill the engines with oil and that was probably what caused the oil pressure to rise and blow the plug out of the port engine. Therefore, they were under no obligation to pay for anything. I told him the starboard engine wasn't overfull. Bullshit it's not, just look on the dipstick, it's way over the full mark, he says. Which it was, but you need to take a closer look, I told him. Wipe the oil off the stick and tell me what you see. He did, and then he got this sheepish look on his face because he knew he opened his mouth before he put his brain in gear. Clearly stamped on the dipstick were the instructions to only check the oil when the engine was running and hot. That was his "oh shit" moment. I fired it up, let it get warm, and had him pull the stick again. Whaddya know, right on the money.

When they found out it was the O-ring that was defective and the wrong size, they did a recall on the engine. We were the first ones to have this happen. The manufacturer did a recall of the motors, replacing the O-rings on them all. They also checked our port main for damage, found none, and totally cleaned and repainted the engine room, just like new.

It was an adventure, and a trial, but we made it back. There are good owners and bad owners, good captains and bad ones. I learned something from each of them, no matter their experience or temperament. That's what I was there for. I took those jobs so I could get the hours to move on to bigger and better boats, but I also took them to learn a thing or two. And whether it was storming outside or smooth as glass, dealing with owners that were drunk or sober as a Mormon in church on Christmas Day, there was always something new to learn.

And then, if you're at it long enough, and you work your ass off, pay attention, sprinkle in some luck, soon you could be the one that's dispensing the lessons. That doesn't mean you stop learning, though. That never stops. Unless you're one of those captains who thinks he's God.

Chapter 7

≈≈≈

Don't Let Your Mouth Write a Check That Your Ass Can't Cash

"We need a new chef," the mate said.

Damn.

It wasn't uncommon to lose a chef in the yachting world. Chefs, in general, are nomadic, temperamental, chaotic, unconventional, and rebellious. They tend to be nocturnal, working all night, partying once the job is done until the sun starts to rise, and then sacking out until the next shift. They're like vampires who roll out their own pasta.

And that's just your garden-variety chef, the kind that works in a city and rents an apartment. But yachting chefs? That's another breed. Those are the group that say, "I love the nights and the chaos and the fast-moving knives, but I'd rather have no fixed address." This sect particularly embraces the kind of pirate life that one gets working on a boat, moving from one Caribbean island to the next, from one coastal town in Florida to the next.

This is to say, even if they were talented and hardworking, you couldn't exactly pencil these guys in for forty years of service and a gold watch at the end.

The bad news was that it meant that I needed a replacement chef.

Even worse, this happened right in the middle of a situation.

I was the captain of a 120-foot Broward. The owner, Doug, had very generously offered his financial consultant, Fredrick, the use of the boat for two weeks for his wedding and honeymoon. We were in Maine for the wedding, but we had only a couple of days to get everything prepared before the big event. Then we were going to Boston the following day to pick up the bride and groom and start their honeymoon cruise. Not sure why they weren't going to stay aboard. Could have been they needed to see some family, or return some gravy boats, or whatever it is newly-weds might do after the big ceremony.

So, I had only a day or two to find a chef who would be diving right into the deep end of the pool.

Picking a chef was part of the job, and the first thing I did was go through my Rolodex of competent people to see if I could find someone who wasn't currently committed. But that's the problem with keeping a list of good people—they were in high demand. It would have been a lot easier to find a total fuckup with an open schedule, but who wants a total fuckup grilling your steaks?

I came up empty. Then I started asking other captains, other owners, other brokers if they knew anyone who might be a good fit. I finally struck gold when I talked to Matt. I'd worked with him in the past, and, if I'd been able to make him a better offer, would have loved to have him running the galley. He was a talented chef who got along well with everyone and really brought everything to the table that a captain would want. But even if he was committed to another job, I still trusted his advice.

"Matty, how's it going?"

"No complaints," he said.

"I'm going to be doing a honeymoon cruise in a couple of days, and I'm in desperate need of a good chef. Know anyone who's looking?"

"Actually, yeah, I know a guy who'd be great. Luke. I'll get you his number."

Under ideal conditions, I like to provide a pretty comprehensive screening process for a new chef. I'd interview him, talk to his references, maybe ask him to cook a meal for the crew to see what kind of food he could make and see how he could get along with everyone else. But time being short, I barely had time to call him up, find out that he was available, and fly him up to Maine.

"If you can get to the boat before the wedding, you're hired."

Problem solved.

But, like everything in life, solving one problem just gives you opportunities to notice new ones.

The new chef, Luke, seemed great. He had plenty of confidence, told me of all the big yachts he'd worked on and the famous clients he'd cooked for, yadda yadda yadda. Chefs have been known to be a wee bit, shall we say, arrogant. Heard that spiel a few times before. Now I was hoping he would deliver and not be just a big bag of wind. I didn't need my sphincter tickled by him blowing smoke up my ass—I just needed a competent chef.

He arrived with a duffel bag full of clothes, a laptop, and a pretty nifty case holding his chef's knives. A chef's knife kit is like a portable résumé and is often the most expensive thing he owns. Luke's laptop probably cost about $800 or so, but I'd wager that knife case held over $2,000 in high-quality steel.

I shook his hand and gave him a quick tour of the boat.

"When do you want me to get started?" he asked.

"Why don't you get settled. Stow your gear, take a look at the galley, get accustomed to where things are and where you want them to be. We'll get underway right after the wedding, so why don't you figure on making breakfast for the crew tomorrow morning, and then we'll talk menus for when the guests arrive."

"Breakfast for just the crew? No guests?" he asked.

"The bridal couple aren't coming on board until two days after the wedding, and we're picking them up in Boston."

"Sounds good."

There were going to be, eventually, a lot of guests. The honeymoon party that we'd be hosting was going to be twelve strong. It was a big boat, with six staterooms for guests, but twelve people was still going to be a mighty strain on the crew. We had only enough real estate to bunk seven crew, unless we started adding new people to sleep on the decks or double up in other people's bunks, and I would have to veto that first idea, and my wife, Mary Anne, would undoubtedly veto the second one.

Usually, you wouldn't want to have more than a 1:1 ratio of guests to crew. We didn't know exactly how hard these guys were going to party, but if they were up all night, the crew would have to be there with them. And no matter how late the diehards went, the crew would have to be ready, bright and early, to greet the first early riser with coffee or tea. Being able to have some crew tasked with late night and some with early morning would put less strain on everyone involved, but for this pleasure cruise, we were just going to have to make the best of it. To handle all twelve guests, it was just going to be me, the first officer, the chief stew, an engineer, the first stew, a deckhand, and the new chef.

The trip from Maine to Boston was uneventful, and Luke did a good job at breakfast. Nothing extraordinary—just bacon, eggs, sausage, toast, and English muffins, but he worked quickly enough, and everything tasted good. He didn't bark at the crew, and nobody played any practical jokes on him, like insisting that the meal include vegan bacon or some shit. Though that would be a great way to haze the chef, not to mention the bacon-loving skipper.

That is something that drives me absolutely nuts, and something mostly on display in younger crew, this weird aura of entitlement. I would interview prospective crew, stews, or deckhands or what have you, and usually, I'd want to see two things: knowledge of the job and the right attitude. But I don't care how much knowledge you have if your attitude revolves entirely around you getting exactly what you want all the time. Yachting may be plush, but it's still a service industry. We serve at the pleasure of our owner and the clients. And it's a lot harder to do that when you have people who insist on serving themselves first.

When I ask someone if they have any special needs or considerations, I'm prepared for things like "I've got asthma" or "I'm allergic to bees" or other things I can deal with. But I sure as hell don't need comments like "I've decided I might be gluten sensitive, so I don't want any bread around me" or "I'm vegan and so I'd prefer that all the crew meals be vegan." That's not how it works. If you don't eat meat, then by all means, don't feel pressured to do so, but we're not tailoring the menu to the junior stew's demands. You're on a raw food diet? Whatever floats your boat, but pack your own carrots because the guests are going to be enjoying grilled salmon. I've had a vegetarian chef work for me, and she made some killer steaks, because cooking for other people is the job. Not everyone gets that. Those that do can work for me. Those that can't—there's always beauty school.

I was glad that Luke seemed capable of doing the job, and on such short notice. After breakfast, he came up to me with a sheepish look on his face.

"Cappy, is it okay if I leave the boat to get rid of some garbage?"

I guess he could have asked the deckhand, but I was glad he wasn't afraid to do his own dirty work. "Fine by me," I said.

He smiled, nodded, and I saw him a few minutes later, walking off the gangway with a couple garbage bags in hand.

That was the last time I saw him. And I do mean the *last* time. I've never seen him since.

Around six, the first officer came to see me.

"Captain, do you know when chow is?"

"Why don't you ask the chef?" I asked.

"I would, but the thing is . . . I can't find him."

Shit.

There could be lots of reasons why the chef wasn't in the galley at dinnertime, and none of them good. Maybe he was sacking out in his bunk, drunk off his ass. It could happen. Maybe he was the kind of guy who liked to put a lot of product in his hair and ended up snapping his neck after slipping on his own hair gel. Maybe he fell overboard. Maybe he hanged himself in a botched attempt at autoerotic asphyxiation. With chefs, it could be anything.

"Let's search the boat," I said.

First, we looked in his cabin. His clothes were still hung up in the closet, still had his duffel bag there. But no sign of Luke. I didn't see his computer, either.

"Okay," I said to the first officer, "what did you do to piss him off?"

"What? Nothing."

"How about anyone else? He make a pass at someone? Get hazed? Lose some money at cards?"

"Far as I know, everyone got on fine with Luke."

I nodded. I certainly hadn't seen any grab-ass or beefing. And there just hadn't been any time for something like that to explode. We'd only picked him up eighteen hours before, and half of that time he'd been sleeping.

We expanded the search and looked in every cabin, every workspace, every crawlspace. Nothing.

Now things were serious. If he wasn't on board, things could have gone really wrong. Even though he had just left the boat to drop off the garbage, it was a bit of a hike from the boat to the Dumpster, maybe a ten-minute hump. There was a chance that, on that long walk, he got injured, maybe mugged. Hell, guys see a nice 120-foot boat come in to the dock, they might think everyone coming off it is rich.

That's when we started making calls.

We called police stations, hospitals, and morgues. Anybody see a skinny Caucasian male with brown hair and a few tats, probably carrying a couple bags of trash and willing to talk at length about demi-glaces and the difference between a coarse chop and a brunoise?

Nobody.

It was a mystery, but not one I could allow to occupy all of my time. Hell, it had already been a crisis when I first hired him back in Maine. Now we needed a second replacement, and with even less time to fill the vacancy! I sent word out to the grapevine, and quickly got a recommendation.

Did this new chef candidate follow his grandma's recipe for delicious handmade ravioli? I had no idea. Shit, I didn't even have time to check if he had a criminal record for sticking a meat thermometer into his last boss's Adam's apple. He had a recommendation, he was available, and he had a pulse. As far as I was concerned, he was perfect. We were getting close to starting the honeymoon cruise, and I had to get someone ASAP while the guests were still off the boat checking out Boston.

Chris, the new Luke, showed up, and impressed the hell out of me by not vanishing in a puff of smoke.

"You take a look at the galley?"

"I sure did. Everything looks good."

"You got all your gear?" I asked.

He held up his chef's knife kit to indicate he did.

That made me think.

"Did you find another one of those lying around the galley anywhere?" I asked.

"Nope. You lose one?"

"I thought someone had."

That's when I realized what happened to Luke. His clothes were still on board, but his knives *weren't*. The only explanation I had was that someone stole them after they figured he'd gone, or he'd taken them off himself. And there was only one good reason why he'd have taken his knives and equipment off the boat: he wasn't planning on coming back.

"That son of a bitch jumped ship," I said. A classic case of someone writing a check with their mouth that their ass couldn't cash.

"What's that?" Chris asked.

"Nothing. Why don't you start getting things squared away the way you like them in the galley, because things are about to go from zero to one hundred."

He nodded, left, and, hopefully, remained on the boat.

I figured Luke had taken a new job. That's why his knives were gone. That's why his computer was gone. He took the expensive stuff, left the thrift-store threads, and bounced.

What an asshole.

These things happened. A guy takes a gig, gets offered more money somewhere else, and he jumps at the chance to make more dough. After all, the best negotiating position one could have was as a man already employed. "Yeah, I'd love to take the job, but I'm already getting paid a fat wad to cook on another boat, so you'd really have to make it worth my while . . ."

It probably would have been more convenient to employ a full-time chef, but a lot of those guys preferred being freelancers. In part, it was for the freedom, but it was also partly because the money was a lot better that way. If a chef took a salary, he might make $75,000 to $100,000 a year, which wasn't bad considering he might not have to pay for rent or food. Still, that broke down to about $200-plus a day. Now, if that same guy wanted to work freelance, he could make up to $500 a day. If a chef got steady work, he could stand to bring in almost $200K per year. Not a bad living, if you could do the work.

And that work wasn't a piece of cake. When you're the chef on a boat, you're working constantly. If the guests plan on being up at 6:00 a.m., then you'd better wake up at 5:30, fire up the cooktop, and have flapjacks and sausages ready by 6:15. When breakfast concludes for everyone around 9:30, that gives you plenty of time to clean the entire galley and start prepping for lunch, served promptly at noon. After the guests depart for a digestive stroll or nap around 2:30, you get to clean things up and prep for dinner, so lobster and filet mignon are ready to go at 6:30. And then, once the last guest finishes her final bite of chocolate lava cake and raspberry sorbet, then you can call it a night, right?

Nope.

After the chef cleans the galley for the final meal, he still has to be on call for the rest of the night. If one of the guests wants a lobster roll at midnight, then the chef has to pry himself out of bed and make it, served with a smile. If a guest has a few drinks and maybe a hit or two from a joint, not that we allow that, but shit happens, and gets the munchies at 2:00 a.m. and absolutely *has* to have some fresh baked chocolate chip cookies, then the chef would be more than happy to accommodate that request. And then breakfast is just a few hours away . . .

So, I was pretty relieved when Chris said that he'd be able to fill in at the last minute.

I just hoped he managed to actually stay on board for more than twenty-four hours.

On our last day in Maine, our owner, Doug, arrived to check out the boat, introduce the guests of honor, and attend the wedding. As soon as the wedding was over, Doug would take off, the happy couple would zoom off to Boston, and then we'd pick them up there a few days later. Doug was a pretty big wheel. He sold his business for about a billion dollars. He was a good owner, and clearly a sweetheart of a guy, since he was just gifting his boat to his financial advisor/friend for nothing. If we had sold that as a charter, it would have cost about 250K. Not a bad wedding present.

"Lee, I want you to show my friend Fredrick a great time. Whatever he wants, he gets," Doug said.

"Can do," I said.

Doug was willing to let them have the crème de la crème, and that was fine with me, since I expected it to be a fairly easygoing sail. Sure, it was two weeks, and the twelve guests would stretch us to full capacity. But Fredrick and his bride, Deborah, were around fifty years old, so I wasn't anticipating twenty-four-hour party people.

Guess you're only as old as you feel.

Fredrick and Deborah married in a traditional Scottish ceremony, with kilts and everything. He seemed a perfectly good sort, the kind of guy who liked to have a good time, but I severely underestimated how much a man in his fifties might like to party. When we got to Boston, I would find out just how much I underestimated the situation.

It was all action all the time. From the moment Doug passed the command to Fredrick, it was nonstop boogie. We took a tour of New England, every day a new city. I had to assume that Fredrick must have been a hell of a financial advisor, because if his vacationing was anything like his work, he did not take days off.

And such was his right. He had command of the boat, could do with it as he pleased. But it would have made life a little easier for me and the crew if he were to take a couple of days at Cape Cod (or Portland or Block Island or Newport or Martha's Vineyard), then the crew could take a little bit of a breather. But when every day meant striking out for a new town, it required sixteen-hour days for everyone on board.

At least everyone was eating well. Restaurants often have the "family meal" they offer as a perk to the staff, a time before the main dining times when the chefs use (often) leftover or unused ingredients to make a meal everyone can enjoy. For that kind of meal, it's typically not the best-of-the-best in terms of what's available. But on this boat? Everyone ate like kings. If Fredrick and Deborah were getting surf and turf, then the crew got surf and turf. If Fredrick and his guests got black truffle risotto, then so did the rest of us.

In part, this was because Doug was a good owner who liked to treat his people well. And in part, this was because it was just logistically impractical to keep two separate menus—one for the guests and one for the crew.

It was delicious, and Chris did a good job. But I have to confess, living high on the hog can get old. Don't get me wrong—I love steak and lobster, but after a dozen meals or so, I find myself longing for some comfort food: some mac and cheese, some chili, some burgers and dogs. Variety is the spice of life.

Fredrick, however, didn't have the same appetites that I did. His tastes ran to the more indulgent, and he never seemed to get tired of it. This was not limited to lobster and filet mignon. He also showed a great love of Cristal champagne. The way Fredrick and his guests were downing that bubbly, you'd have thought he was an investor in the company. And that stuff isn't cheap. Sure, Doug made it clear that Fredrick was to get anything he wanted, but I'd check in with him pretty regularly, just to let him know how the trip was going. As the honeymoon continued, and proceeded at the same breakneck pace, he started getting a little concerned.

A bottle of Cristal usually goes for at least a couple hundred per, and we were getting the good stuff, tipping the scales at about $1,200 per bottle. We'd buy it by the case, and each case would be six bottles, so every case was over $7,000 in champagne. When Doug saw how much of it was getting consumed, he started feeling a little less hospitable.

"You sure Freddy's drinking all that champagne? Any chance someone is just billing me for the Cristal and blowing the money on personalized Patriots jerseys or something? Or does Freddy really have a problem?"

I didn't think Doug was serious. Though, for some people on a boat, even one with internet and a gym and a SatPhone, liquor could be a tempting way to entertain and escape. Sometimes, a chef would buy something for himself and try to pass it off as ship's stores. If you found a bottle of vodka behind the corn flakes, you knew you had a problem.

Those kinds of problems could really spiral out of control. I was once going on a quick run to pick up a boat, called the *Sea Ghost*, a nice 135-foot Fed ship. This particular vessel had been owned by Nicolas Cage, but Nic had run afoul of the IRS, and in order to pay the taxman's bill, he'd been forced to liquidate some islands and castles and boats. Motivated seller. It was my job to report to Connecticut and captain the boat over to Florida, where I'd deliver it to the new owner.

We were just operating on a skeleton crew since we didn't plan on doing any fancy sightseeing or chartering. Just pick up the boat, move it from A to B, drop off the keys, and mission accomplished. Unfortunately, even though it was a skeleton crew, one of the bones on that skeleton had at least a few fractures in it.

One of the engineers, Dick, was a drunk. And I don't mean that he liked to have a few too many glasses of wine with dinner, I mean that he'd pour himself a tumbler full of vodka and then pass out with the drink still in his hand. Just because vodka looks clear as water doesn't mean I didn't figure out his little game. My first clue, of course, was that he was unconscious during the day. Always a red flag. Another red flag was his eyeballs, almost literally. His eyes looked like a road map of the Chicago business Loop. He really saw the world through rose-colored eyeballs.

He wasn't my hire, and I couldn't fire him. It wasn't my job to staff the boat, just to get it where the owner wanted it. The problem was, I couldn't have Dick stand watches, so everyone just had to take on more work and more responsibility. Instead of him standing a four-hour watch, everyone else would just have to add an hour to his own watch.

I tried to make some kind of dent in the damage that Dick could do by policing up his cabin. The room looked like a recycling plant. Just bottles everywhere. I don't think the guy even had any clothes, just the ones he was wearing on his back, because all the available space he lived in was devoted to vodka bottles in various stages of emptiness. The guy didn't have a drinking problem—the only problem he had was when he couldn't find a drink.

The only job that I'd allow him to perform was to top off the oil and swap over the generators. It wasn't brain surgery, but it was still important, because if he screwed up, he could overfill the tanks, and then we'd end up trailing oil and have to deal with the Coast Guard on our ass. As a safeguard against him confusing the oil tanks with his mouth and the oil canisters with vodka and just dumping it all in, I always ordered the first mate to accompany him and make sure he was doing it properly. That's why I usually had a drinking rule on the boat: eight hours from bottle to throttle.

At first, I tried to talk to Dick, explain to him that he was endangering the boat and the crew and that he was destroying his own life, but he just wouldn't have it. He was one of those drunks that would just talk over everyone. He was a man immune to logic, impervious to argument, blind to reason.

"Dick, you have to get a hold of—"

"I do my job, and my job is to be an engineer, and not to be the head of the damn Women's Christian Temperance Movement."

"I'm not saying that you need to have some kind of religious—"

"You can't tell me how to live my life! I can eat what I want and drink what I want and read what I want and watch whatever shows I want! Because this is America! In case you forgot!"

"I know what country we're—"

"It's not Russia! You can't be Big Brother! When I was . . ."

And so it went. I couldn't get him to stop drinking, so I put a babysitter on him and reduced the scope of the damage he could do. Four days later, we slipped into the docks, and I handed over the keys.

The manager and broker took possession of the boat, and I took the opportunity to tell them about Dick.

"I know, I know," the broker said. "He's always like that."

They knew?! They knew and they hadn't fired him? It was like they were begging for a catastrophic accident or a catastrophic lawsuit. But hey—not my circus, not my monkeys. We went from point A to point B, everyone lived, and it was a good crossing, so I just had to chalk it up as a W.

This is a long way of saying that hitting the bottle could be a big problem, either from the perspective of having someone on a boat you couldn't trust or from the perspective of keeping someone as your financial consultant that you couldn't trust. But from what I saw, our bridegroom Freddy wasn't a drunk—just a guy who liked to party.

"I guess Freddy just really takes his leisure time seriously," I said.

"Maybe see if you can taper things down a bit," Doug suggested. Doug wasn't cheap, but there are limits to how far you can push a host's generosity before you have to reclassify that as taking advantage of someone.

Maybe that was just the kind of guy that Freddy was. That's what I'd started calling him. Because Fredrick is a cultured, sophisticated professional, and Freddy is an aging adolescent mooch. Maybe that's how he became a successful financial guy in the first place—he was never going to set limits for himself if no one was going to impose them on him. He certainly seemed comfortable asking for the moon.

After we'd cruised around New England a bit, Freddy decided he didn't want to miss fireworks on the Fourth of July. That sounded reasonable, so I asked him where he might want to check things out.

"Let's motor back into Boston Harbor. They put on a good show."

There's no denying that. Still, it was kind of a big ask. Thousands of boats flood those harbors to watch the fireworks show, and it was a real bitch to navigate through it. Boats weren't allowed to drop an anchor, so we would have to be constantly running the engine and trying to maneuver so we didn't drift too far or run into any of the other ten thousand boats.

But what really held me back was that we just displaced too much water, and it was too shallow right up close to the fireworks. We couldn't get to where he wanted us to be, and Freddy didn't like that too much. But I wasn't going to beach the boat just so he could get a better view of the fireworks. It pissed him off, but it probably saved us a lot of ill will from the rest of the boating world. We were a big boat at 120 feet, and I was glad that I wouldn't have to suffer with the guilt of dozens of other smaller boats hating our guts because we were this huge yacht blocking their view. We were able to snuggle up right next to the docks at Yacht Haven Grande, and Freddy still got a great show, so he had nothing to complain about, even if he sure gave it the ol' college try.

Finally, we'd made it through the honeymoon. We'd visited four states, consumed a vineyard's worth of champagne, a cove's worth of lobster, and shown the newlyweds a pretty good time. And how did they thank us for our hospitality and our sixteen-hour days?

They stiffed us.

As Freddy was headed off the boat, he said, "Let me just go get the car and pull it around." Well, maybe there was something magic about that particular gangplank, because Freddy must have fallen into the same twilight zone that Luke had also disappeared into. Never saw either of those guys ever again. He got his car, Deborah ran to catch up, and then he was gone.

This was a first for me. While I'd received some shitty tips in my time, I'd never been given the total bagel before. Now, a trip like this would normally cost a client, as a high-end charter, about 250K. And while Doug wasn't billing Freddy for the trip, I'd assumed that he understood that tipping was customary. If someone provides an open bar at a party, you still tip the bartenders. If you use a gift certificate at a restaurant, you still tip the servers. And even if you didn't pay for the charter, we were still hoping for a standard gratuity, which in the yachting game was somewhere between 10 percent to 20 percent. But we didn't get the $50,000 at the high end, or even the $25,000 bare minimum. And that 10 percent tip is something you'd get even if you really screwed up, serving PB&Js for dinner, not knowing how to get to certain ports, that kind of thing. And this guy was getting first-class everything! Turns out that bare minimum can be a lot more bare than 10 percent, and we got the total shaft. Thanks for the cruise—now you can all go fuck yourselves.

Some might argue that Freddy shouldn't have had to pay the gratuity because he was gifted the cruise in the first place and, therefore, shouldn't have to pay anything. But if you can't tip seven people who busted their asses 24/7 without a single day off for two weeks, then you just have to say "no" to that cruise. It's a gift you can't afford.

It made me want to run down that road to try to warn Freddy's new bride that she might want to rethink this partnership. If he was going to show as much generosity to her as he did to my crew, it might end up being a short marriage. But, hey—he did wear a kilt to the wedding, so maybe she had some inkling of what she might be getting into.

That was a pretty bracing splash of cold water.

Maybe we weren't the only beneficiaries of Freddy's lack of social skills, because Doug stopped working with him not too long after that. At least he got a nice cruise as his severance.

Still, all's well that ends well. And once we finished the honeymoon charter, we finally got confirmation on what happened to our missing chef. I got a call from Matty, the guy who had referred him in the first place.

"I found your boy," he said.

"Who?"

"Luke. The disappearing chef."

"Aliens get him?" I asked.

"He said he had to run away. Said everyone was making life miserable for him and he couldn't take it anymore."

"Couldn't take it? He was only on the boat for less than a day! And half of that was sleeping."

"Yeah, it's obviously bullshit, but a man needs to protect his reputation. He ended up taking another job for more dough."

"If his reputation was what he was worried about," I said, "then he shouldn't have walked off my boat without a word of explanation. Guy gets a wild hair up his butt crossways, not much I can do about that. Total lack of integrity. He definitely let his mouth write a check his ass couldn't cash. As far as I'm concerned, I'll never work with him again," I said. And I'm not shy about telling the truth about someone like that when I'm asked.

"You and me both," Matty said.

Not the best cruise I ever had. A chef disappeared, the clients stiffed us on the tip, and my boss saw all his Cristal go down the toilet. But sometimes, that was just the way of things in the glamorous world of yachting. You can have sunny days that still kill you. You can work alongside talented people who still make you want to throw them through the window. It may be an interesting line of work, but a lot of the time, it's still work.

And thank God for it.

Chapter 8

~~~~~~~~~~~

You Have One Shot at Integrity

There's a lot of money in the yachting world, and with that money comes a lot of opportunities for abuse. Sometimes, that's just how the rules are made, and you have to live by them, even if you don't agree with them. Sometimes, you make a stand against it because that's your code. That's how I live my life. You only have one shot at integrity, and you can't blow it all just to make a couple of dollars. Some do, as is their right, but those aren't the kind of guys I choose to work with. Just because someone's not going to miss a dollar bill, or a stack of them, doesn't mean it's okay to steal. The line is clear to me, but I can see how some people find it, to their eye, a bit more fuzzy.

I didn't come from a lot of money. My first car was a 1955 Chevy Bel Air that I bought for $50 when it was twelve years old. You could see through the floorboards because the body was all rusted out, and it belched smoke like it was on fire, but it got me to my job at the bakery where I was glad to earn 75 cents an hour. A four-hour shift would get me a shirt soaked with sweat and a nice $3 for the day. So that car, even though it was a piece of shit, still cost me seventeen days of scrubbing caramelized sugar off some seriously pre-Teflon pans. In the most basic and honest definition of the word, I *earned* the money for that car. Back in the good old days, when things weren't always good.

It's with that perspective that I would marvel at what some people might label the excessive, or opulent, or pampered lives of some of the people in the yachting world. To afford a yacht in the first place, you had to have some deep pockets. With pockets that deep, some people are just never going to fish around in them for a lost quarter.

One time in Baltimore, I got a call from an owner who wanted a suckling pig for his dinner on New Year's Eve. No problem—it was a specialty request, but not tremendously exotic. But wait—there's more. It couldn't just be any suckling pig, it had to be the same kind that they'd had for the first time visiting New Zealand. Only a New Zealand suckling pig would do. And this request came down the pike on December 30.

"Can do," I said.

I'd have to find a way to make it happen, but who's got that number in their Rolodex? The contact for acquiring delicious pigs in New Zealand? That's just the nature of the beast. I'd figure it out, but it was going to cost. Specialty requests cost money. Rush requests cost extra. And guarantees for all the above just add to the tally. But it was important for the man to get what he wanted, and it was my job to do exactly that. My thinking generally is that very difficult jobs I do immediately, and the impossible jobs just take a little extra thought. Especially when working for people that live by the motto "*No* is never a word I want to hear."

Now, if you buy a suckling pig from a butcher or specialty purveyor, you could probably get one on the low end for about $150. If you go for something a bit higher in quality, the price jumps to maybe $400. But if you want something of high quality, and you want it from the other side of the world, and you want it fast, the costs are going to go up. How much did we end up paying to get what the owner wanted?

About $4,000.

And we did it. We got exactly what he wanted, we got it delivered on time, and it was delicious, or so I was told. It basically cost the amount of booking a couple of seats on a commercial airliner, but for a guy with millions or even billions to spend, four grand to him is what I spend on bubblegum, and I don't torture myself over how much money I'm going to spend on a pack of gum.

Another owner had a special project that would have made a normal guy flinch but didn't make him bat an eyelash, nor should it have. He wanted to get a new dining room table, and for the material on top, he wanted a single, solid slab of onyx.

I didn't even know you could buy an onyx slab for a dining table. I knew you could buy wood, or glass, or steel, and if you wanted to do stone, maybe someone could do marble or granite or soapstone. But onyx? I'd only heard that as a material people used in jewelry, not furniture. If I wanted to buy some onyx earrings, I could probably find some at Macy's between $100 and $1,000, depending on how flashy I was feeling. But an entire table? A table that was supposed to seat twelve people? That was a lot of onyx. And it wasn't just the raw weight—this guy wanted it to be in a single slab. So even though it might have been easier or cheaper to find two or more pieces and then just glue them together, the owner didn't want any seams to mar the table's surface.

So, I made a few calls. Eventually, I found a stone purveyor who was able to find the slab I was looking for, but it wasn't cheap. The slab alone cost $25,000. If we were going to install the slab into a house with a wide-open front door, then maybe the costs would have ended there. But on a yacht, everything is more complicated. Unlike a mansion, the roads for a yacht go to the marina, not to the numbers on a mailbox. In order to get that slab in the boat and set it down nice and gentle, we needed to commission a crane and the personnel capable of using it. We needed to hire craftsmen who could install it properly. At the end of the day, that tabletop ended up costing the owner $50,000.

And hell, it looked gorgeous.

Though one of the big questions was always, How long is that going to last? Even though a lot of owners visit their yachts only a few times a year, they're remarkably susceptible to environmental fatigue. One time, an owner came on board, looked around for a bit, gestured at the dining room chairs, and said, "I'm sick of looking at these—let's change it." And it wasn't like the guy was pointing to chairs with warped wood or couches in the salon with red wine stains on the upholstery. He just got bored with seeing the same thing. And this boredom could set in quickly—often in under two years.

So, these gorgeous dining room chairs had to go. "I hate them—go buy new ones," he said. And that was that. No discussion, no auction, just make them go away. But the chairs *were new*. No one had ever sat in them before. "Just get rid of them," the owner said. Those chairs cost about $1,000 each, and we ended up just asking the crew if they wanted to take them home. It was that or give them to the Salvation Army. Here's a pro tip if you want to become a professional furniture flipper: follow the stuff that comes flying off a yacht. It's a good way to buy a thousand-dollar chair for $50.

One of the biggest drivers of change on a boat would be a change in the owner's personal life. If the guy got a new wife or a new girlfriend, it was time for a makeover. The new girlfriend didn't want to sleep on the same linens as the old girlfriend. Or she didn't want to use the same towels. Or she didn't want to sleep in the same bed. Or eat off the same table. Or be cooled by the same generators. Whatever might cause her emotional distress or mental anguish, that would just have to go, even if that change meant replacing all the carpets or the upholstery or the navigation system (not typical, that last one).

It wasn't always big-ticket items like 50K tabletops. Sometimes it was something as simple as linens. But even then, simple doesn't mean cheap. Sometimes, we'll be told to get bedding for all the cabins. But they don't just want sheets from JC Penney. They want 1,200-thread-count sheets, and those sheets need to be Egyptian cotton. Because, they say, it's the best. And that's an easy get.

They're not always so easy.

Just about everyone has sheets, but not everyone has rare art.

One time, an owner looked at a space on the wall and said, "I've got to fill that with something." But he didn't plan on just slapping up a poster from the movie *Donnie Darko* or Einstein sticking his tongue out. This wasn't a college dorm room. He wanted Art with a capital *A*. He wanted a Pollock or a Warhol or a Kandinsky. For his boat.

It should be noted that one doesn't just purchase an original Jackson Pollock and that's the end of it. A Pollock can cost up to $200 million, and that's without the frame. Even a lesser Pollock, at $50 million, is both a lot of money to spend and just the first stage in an elite art purchase. After all, news of an art sale of that magnitude will be reported. That's, to a large degree, one of the key factors motivating the purchase in the first place. People will know. People will be impressed. So, in addition to the art itself, the owner also had to purchase security.

In order to protect the owner's purchases, we installed a top-flight security system. It had pressure-sensitive pads on the deck to alert us if anything larger than a hedgehog tried to get on board. To monitor all the public spaces in the boat, we also had closed-circuit TVs equipped with night-vision lenses, and these were complemented by heat sensors in the gangways. Nobody was getting on the boat without the security detail being aware of it.

But that wasn't all.

After buying the painting, after installing the $100,000 security system, after all of that, the owner still had one more purchase to make.

He had to buy a duplicate of the painting.

The duplicate itself wasn't cheap. This had to be convincing. It couldn't just be some print he bought at the Museum of Modern Art's gift shop, mass produced and printed by some high-end laser printer. This had to really look like the original, it had to be oil on canvas, it had to have three-dimensional layering of paint, and be produced by an actual painter intimately familiar with the original artist's work and techniques. That alone cost a pretty penny. And it was well spent.

After all, he was spending $50 million on a work of art—who's going to hang that on a wall? Things happen to walls. But for an investment like that, he put the painting in a vault.

But if the painting was in a vault in some bank, then why the need for all the security?

Because the painting was purchased as a way to impress. It's part of how the owner tells a story. The story is "I'm important, I have great taste, and I have quite a bit of money." That story isn't going to be convincingly told without a few props. One doesn't just put an original Pollock up on a bulkhead and call it a day. To really sell that story, you need the additional security, all the technical tools, and staff. If you're going to spend $50 million to tell a story, you can spend a million more to sell it.

This is all to say that where there's a lot of money, there's a lot of money to spend. And where money can flow, corruption has a way of working its way into the picture.

Refits are expensive. This provides opportunities both legitimate and illegitimate.

When a boat gets a refit, it means getting a tune-up to the hundredth degree. It means fixing, restoring, cleaning, modifying, customizing, or otherwise improving a boat, exterior and/or interior. For big boats, this can require a lot of work.

And a lot of dollars.

There are lots of people who can do the work. There are different contractors who would love to resurface the decks or paint the superstructure. There are plenty of interior decorators who would love to throw out hundreds of thousands of dollars in furniture and replace it with brand-new cabinets, tables, and art. The captain holds a great deal of power in making these decisions. He's the one who solicits bids and talks to the specialists who could do the work.

There's a lot of money riding on those kinds of decisions. Enough money, in fact, that a few thousand directed to the right person might not be seen as an expense, but as insurance to guarantee a high-paying job. Some people call it "perks," but I call it what it is: a kickback. Sometimes, an owner will take the boat into the yard for a refit, and before the work even starts, the crew might notice that the captain is now driving around in a brand-new pickup truck. These jobs could cost millions of dollars, so someone giving the captain a bag with $20,000 in cash might seem like a real bargain.

Not to me.

I've always felt that a captain should make decisions like that based on who can do the best job, not who can be the quickest to fill a gym bag with twenties. I've been in those situations. On more than one occasion, I've been handed an envelope with a bid in it only to find out there's more in that envelope.

"There's a twenty-thousand-dollar check in there for you, too, Cap," the bidder said.

"Why don't you just take the 20K out of the bottom line for the boss," I replied.

"We really want to win this bid," he said.

"You have a better chance of winning the bid by thinking about the owner's financial situation, and not mine," I said.

Not everyone agrees. One owner I knew just felt that this sort of thing was a kind of bonus for the captain. He thought that there were lots of good companies out there, and if soliciting a bribe got his captain a new truck or a down payment on a summer house, then what was wrong with that? But that's just never the way that I've seen things. I'm paid to do my job by the owner—I'm not paid by a contractor with his own agenda. If you keep the conflicts of interest to a minimum, your life gets simpler and easier.

Captains aren't the only ones targeted for this kind of scam. Chefs wield remarkable power on ship as well. If an owner decides that he wants to modernize or upgrade the galley, he'll seek input from the captain, but he'll lean heavily on the expertise of the chef to make many of those decisions. And those kinds of decisions can prove incredibly lucrative to a company selling ovens, walk-in freezers, grills, cooktops, and any other appliances that could be on the acquisition to-do list. As a result, a kitchen supply company might offer a chef a few thousand dollars to steer business its way. A good chef should simply make the decision based on what's best for the boat, but some put their own pocketbooks first. If a chef switches all his knives from Crate & Barrel to Wüsthof right after a big upgrade, it might be a sign he took a kickback.

Big-ticket items like pricy name-brand appliances aren't the only way that a chef could wield the power of the owner's black card. Stocking up on booze for the season can be an incredibly hefty bar tab. We never want to run on empty at the bar, and so we'll often buy up to $100,000 worth of alcohol to top off before the season starts. With those kinds of numbers, a less ethical chef might ask around for $5,000 in "consultation fees" before deciding on which distributor will satisfy his needs. From my perspective, you just never want to be in the position where you're stocking cheapie Popov vodka instead of Grey Goose or Hamm's beer instead of Guinness because that's how the distributor was able to fill the order while still affording their payoff.

Some people think they're entitled to dip in. After all, the owner isn't the one who has to pay for it, right? But the thing is, any time you're making decisions based on something other than "What's the best way to do your job," things can get missed.

And that's where you can run into big trouble.

I was working this one boat when things didn't go the right way. I'm not saying that this was necessarily because of bribes or kickbacks (though I'm not saying that wasn't a factor). I'm just saying what can happen if people don't keep their eyes on the ball at all times.

I was going to be taking charge of the boat, a 165-footer, once it finished its refit in Europe. The refit was pretty pricy—about 4.5 million euros ($5.5 million). We could probably have done it in the US for maybe $2 million, but the owner wanted it done in Europe, and the owner gets what he wants. Part of the refit was that we were going to get the boat painted, which ended up costing the owner 1.7 million euros.

It certainly seemed like a high price tag, but keep in mind that painting a boat of that size isn't a simple job. You don't just call your friends over to the marina, get a few rollers, and spread a coat or two of True Value Navajo White all over the hull. Painting is a very technical, precise job. Before you even get to the painting, a painter has to do a ton of prep. They erect massive scaffolding around the boat, then construct a tent over the scaffolding. Either that, or they dock the boat inside a big shed. Not only does that protect the boat from rain and wind, but it also protects people from the boat. Often, there's a lot of scraping and sanding when a boat is prepped for paint, and that residue can be inhaled, so the tent or shed keeps all that in, and the air is filtered before it can be released outside of the tarp.

The prep team goes over the hull, and if they want a new coat of paint, they sand off the old one. Then they search the hull for any dings, dents, or abrasions before sanding or pounding or polishing them off. This all takes thousands of hours, and the paint hasn't even been applied yet!

As part of the prep, the painter needs to remove every bolt and screw that covers the deck plating. Every screw, every doorknob, every cleat, everything that isn't the superstructure needs to be removed, marked, and catalogued. For that boat, it was about 100,000 screws. And before the screws could go back in, they all had to be coated, individually, in Tef-Gel. This gel allows someone to insert and remove screws from a hull. Often, different things on a ship are made from different materials. So, the hull might be steel, the screws might be stainless steel, and the superstructure might be aluminum. When you have two different materials interacting with each other, it can cause electrolysis, which can create bubbles in the metal. Not a desirable outcome. All 100,000 screws had to have Tef-Gel applied with a toothbrush. If each application of Tef-Gel just took a single second, and the guy coating it never took a break or slowed down, it would take about twenty-eight man-hours just to coat every screw on the boat.

Then, finally, came the paint. But . . . not quite. First, the workspace needed to be adjusted to the right conditions. The temperature had to be kept constant, at about 65 degrees, so there wasn't any expansion or contraction of the materials. The interior walls were washed with cascading water so that even minuscule contaminants were kept away. Even the air was accounted for—inside that tarp, the air pressure was kept higher than the outside air pressure. That meant, even with people coming in and going out, the air on the inside pushed out that contaminated outside air. Just walking in to work on the job, people felt a slight punch of air against them.

At that point, the painter could apply a show coat. This was not "show" in the sense of a show pony, but in a "show me what's wrong with this picture." The show coat, usually blue or green, helps reveal any flaw or irregularity on the hull. Those were fixed by using a fairing compound, then re-sanded and primed, and finally the finish coat was applied. Another inspection would take place, maybe it passed, maybe it didn't. If it didn't, then they would re-sand and reshoot the boat again until it was right. Then all the screws were reinserted and the doorknobs replaced. If everything was done right, the exterior paint would be so brilliant, it would literally reflect the water.

Problem was, for me, that this particular boat had orange peels in a lot of places. Orange peels happen because the paint was applied improperly so that the exterior wasn't smooth and uniform. As a result, you get the subtle dimpling of an orange peel.

I didn't oversee the refit and painting of the boat. It was just a delivery job for me, bringing the boat to the owner. That said, even if you're just the messenger, you do not want to be the guy handing over a boat covered with orange peel that just got a 1.7-million-euro paint job. Especially when it should have cost only about a million euros at most. You shouldn't do a crap job, and you shouldn't overcharge, but you sure as hell shouldn't do *both* and not expect someone to notice.

You get that orange peel by someone screwing up, usually when a painter uses incorrect technique on the job. For instance, he might use too much paint in a single coat, or he might spray at an angle rather than perpendicular to the surface, or he might not have enough pressure in the spray gun, etc. I saw it and thought, *No way*. You pay a lot of money for a job, you want to see perfection. Someone put on that orange peel finish, and that was a mistake. Not smoothing it with some fairing compound was a second mistake. Someone else checked it, saw that it wasn't perfect, and said, "Eh—good enough," and that was a third mistake. I said they should sand it down and try it again. And there were a few other things, problems with the boat that I pointed out to the owner, signs that someone either let something slip or was trying to pull one over on him. I thought they should try again. The owner, on the other hand, disagreed.

See, the owner had been without his boat for a year while it was getting the refit. And after a year, he didn't want to hear that the boat was going to need to go back to the yard, get sanded down, get looked over, have all the screws removed, get repainted, have all those screws covered in Tef-Gel again, and everything put into working order. That's another three months to a year of work. Who had the patience for that? Instead, he said, "Let me just take it, and we'll have them redo it the next time we're in the yard."

Suuuurrrre. Of course, they'll hop to when we come strolling in, in another year or two. They were happy enough to agree to such a proposal, because they knew they'd never have to follow through with it. And sure enough, when he did bring it back, they told him it had been out of the yard too long and that they couldn't really guarantee the work at that point. And why would they? If you buy a car and see a scratch, that's on the dealership. You buy a car, see a scratch, then drive it around town for a year, and *then* bring it back? Good luck getting the dealer to pay for it.

This is to say that even when there's a lot of money on the table, and even when you go to a reputable professional who has performed work at a very high level for many years, there's still room for error and corruption. Why open the door to crippling conflicts of interest by allowing kickbacks and bribes? The guy offering the kickback isn't doing it because you love money—he's doing it because *he* loves money. Once that payoff is made, he's not just going to see that kickback as a gift to a capable business-man—it's a loss that needs to be recovered. And where's the first place he's going to try to make up that loss? On the job he just paid the kickback for. He'll try to cut corners, hire less qualified people, buy sub-prime materials, pad the billings. When some-one's getting a little extra, someone else is sure as hell getting shortchanged.

Do your job and demand others to do the same, and you'll do all right.

Of course, it can go the other way, too. Money doesn't always flow from the vendors to the captains or the chefs. Sometimes, the owners like to get in on that kind of action. If bribes are a way to grease the skids, owners aren't immune from wanting to get a little greasy every now and again.

One time, I saw an owner come to visit his boat while it was getting a refit, and as a way to encourage everyone's best efforts, he handed out one hundred dollars to every painter, electrician, and carpenter working his boat that day. And it worked. Those guys really wanted to put in a top effort for that owner. Added to that, news spreads fast at the docks, and lots of other painters and electricians and carpenters heard about the high-roller who liked throwing out bonus money.

But it wasn't a popular move with everyone.

The guys who managed the yard weren't too happy with that kind of maneuver. Sure, it improved morale for the guys working that job, but as a result, everyone else stopped their jobs and tried to get on at our boat.

"Need an extra carpenter?" someone would ask.

"No, we've got a full crew," the foreman would reply.

"Okay. I'll just hang around in case you need someone."

These guys had other jobs they were being paid to do, and now they couldn't figure out a reliable schedule because everyone wanted to bail on what they were doing and come help refit my boat. So, the owner ended up dropping $2,000, which was nothing to him, and set the whole yard on fire with guys thinking they were going to be courtside when he came back to make it rain. Guys should just do their jobs and not get greedy, but everyone likes money.

Some people might argue that this is just practical economics at its most basic. You make a little bribe, offer a little kickback, and you get what you want. In return, the person paying gets what he wants. Everyone's happy, and the money helps identify how much things are genuinely worth. Adam Smith's invisible hand in action.

But what happens when the money makes things *worse?*

The Eastern Seaboard is spotted with lovely towns where the rich folks like to party for the weekend during the summer.

Sometimes, those wealthy weekenders like to travel by boat. If they wanted to dock their boats at the pier, they would have to speak to the dockmaster. The dockmaster is the person in charge of the waterfront. He or she is the one who got to decide who stayed and who went. For at least one, whom I'll call Rob, one of the things that helped him make those decisions was how amenable a captain might be to contributing to his favorite charity, which we might call the Rob Retirement Fund. It was a kind of art preservation society, for Rob was keenly interested in collecting the portraits of dead presidents. If you wanted a slip, it might cost you $1,000 in cash for a single night, plus your normal docking rate.

Some might argue that this simply clarified who wanted the dock space the most. The person who paid proved he was the one in most desperate need, and this way, the slips were allocated in the most fair and judicious fashion.

But the thing was, if Rob didn't get the payments he demanded, those slips would remain empty. Does that seem like smart economics? The boaters didn't benefit, since they couldn't dock, and the town wouldn't benefit, since now there were fewer people entering the town to eat at its restaurants, shop at its antique shops, and find other ways to spend their money. The only person who really seemed to be benefitting was Rob.

Still, his defenders would say he was just doing his job. He kept order, he discouraged the riffraff, that kind of thing. However, when Rob found himself eating at a nice restaurant and there was a captain in the vicinity, he would never have to pay his own tab. It was almost always taken care of. How does the dockmaster getting a free dinner help the town? The straight-up truth is that he ran the harbor his way because he liked money, something certainly not unique to Rob.

But, in some places, there are a few things that even money can't buy.

Where there's glamour, there are yachts. And there are fewer places as glamorous as Cannes, France, for its film festival or Monaco for the Grand Prix, one of the most prestigious races in all of motorsport. People come from all over the world to attend these events, but it's not exactly open to everyone. You need to have a lot of money, and you need to have celebrity.

It's kind of fascinating how the economies of glamour work. Take the Cannes Film Festival. If you want to dock at a slip, it's going to cost you. You'd be smart to give the harbormaster a nice "gratuity" if you want to be able to get a plum space, a tip in the neighborhood of $100,000. A very nice neighborhood, indeed. Otherwise, instead of getting a nice slip right at dockside, be prepared to drop anchor in the bay and send an A-list passenger landward in a dingy.

But money won't buy everything. You can't just be rich—you have to be a celebrity. And not just some art-house darling like Darren Aronofsky or TV star like Jim Parsons. You need to be A-list all the way: George Clooney, Oprah Winfrey, or Steven Spielberg. If you don't have someone in that weight class, it's not going to be easy.

And this is where things get interesting. Hypothetically, let's take someone like David Geffen. Geffen is one of the biggest music and film producers in the entertainment industry. In music, he owned the label that produced albums with John Lennon, Elton John, Cher, the Eagles, Aerosmith, Guns N' Roses, and Nirvana. In film, he founded the studio DreamWorks SKG with Steven Spielberg and Jeffrey Katzenberg (the *S* and the *K* to his *G*), producing such films as *Gladiator*, *American Beauty*, *Shrek*, and *A Beautiful Mind*. He has an estimated net worth of $6.5 billion. He is, to put it mildly, a pretty big wheel. But he could walk down almost any street in America and never get recognized. A gazillionaire and no one would know who he was.

And he might not stand a chance of getting a slip in Cannes.

George Clooney, on the other hand, is a big, recognizable star. You know he's not walking down any street without getting mobbed. And he's not doing too bad in terms of money, with about $500 million in the bank. But he doesn't own a giga-yacht, because that would wipe out half his net worth. So, Clooney can't get dockside because he doesn't have a boat, and Geffen might get rejected because he's not a big enough celebrity. So, what do they do? Geffen asks his friend George if he might want to be a guest on his boat, and George kindly accepts, and someone pays the harbormaster a six-figure tip, and they can pull right onto the dock without having to drop the hook in the harbor like some lesser-known billionaire might have to.

In a lot of ways, it doesn't seem fair. But there's a reason why a good number of the harbormasters in Monaco drive Ferraris and have a phone full of selfies accompanied by the world's most famous people.

And it isn't limited to the harbormaster. Once you're finally in port, you're going to want to have a good time. The owner and his guests are going to want to eat, drink, and be merry. But so does everyone else with a boat. That means that lots of purveyors are getting orders for mussels, for steaks, for wine. The chef will get a message that his order is in, but that he's at the bottom of the list.

"I need that case of wine tonight. It's Harrison Ford's favorite! You can't get it in America!"

"Oh, I understand completely. If you want to move up the list, you could pay for *express* service."

It's not the chef's dime, after all, but it's his job to make it happen.

"Sure. Add ten percent for yourself. But get it here this afternoon."

"No problem."

When you've got the cash, there's never a problem.

~~~~~

It can be a cruel world out there. Everyone is looking to make a buck, everyone is looking to get ahead, and some things can just drive you crazy. Some folks will work their whole lives in a West Virginia coal town, digging coal and barely putting food on the table, while a few miles away, some rich kid is born who inherits a couple of billion dollars and never wears the same underwear twice. Even among the rich, there are different strata. Some guys are buying yachts and then feel insecure when they see someone else with a helipad on theirs.

It's amazing the things people will do when they have the money. I knew one guy who owned a very nice 40-foot center console, but he didn't want it to get polluted by people using it for a tender when they chartered his mega-yacht. So, he spent $500,000 on an Intrepid, a 12-meter tender, just to use when the big boat was on charter. That's like buying a Lexus just to keep around for when your brother-in-law is in town, because you don't want him driving your Bentley. He had the money, and that's how he wanted to spend it.

Or take PJ. He would charter a boat for his friends to use, even though he owned his own boat. He'd pay $100,000 just to charter a boat so his friends wouldn't get their Manolo Blahnik shoeprints all over his deck.

But that's their business. That's not something I have to worry about at all. Just because some guy has the money to spend on two boats doesn't mean he'd be happy if I skimmed a little off him with some creative expense reports. If an owner is willing to pay a million bucks to refit his boat, that doesn't mean I get license to pocket $20,000 in kickbacks. Someone being richer than me doesn't mean I have to be miserable. Even with billionaires buying tropical islands and castles, you can still make a nice life for yourself. You can be happy driving a Mustang even if someone else is driving a McLaren. You can be happy eating a porterhouse steak even if someone else is chowing down on lobster stuffed with caviar. Taking a kickback might get me a hair closer to those kinds of deep pockets, but I'll never do it, because you only get one chance at integrity. That's worth a lot more to me than a shoebox full of cash.

Some things, you just can't buy.

Chapter 9

≈≈≈≈≈≈

There Is No Dumbass Vaccine

I f you're working with a bad captain, it's rough, but at least he's a captain. He has to know something to be there in the first place, and that knowledge can be helpful. It's not always the same with an owner. To own a boat, the only thing he needs to know is the location of his checkbook. You can't argue seamanship with someone who doesn't know a square knot from a half hitch, or effective staff management with someone who inherited his fortune. One of the biggest problems you can possibly face when dealing with an owner, or anyone, is a disagreement with someone who doesn't know what he doesn't know.

Such was my problem when I took a new assignment, becoming the captain of a custom-made 140-footer. I liked the boat. It had five staterooms and good lines, and I figured it would be a decent job to captain her through charter season. But there were problems. One issue: there were two owners. That's not uncommon. Yachts cost a hell of a lot of money, and sometimes, to avoid the full impact of the sticker shock, guys like to have a partner. Or an owner will know that he won't need the boat 365 days of the year and might as well have someone else be able to use it. Still, having multiple owners can also mean multiple agendas, where one guy will vote going in one direction and his partner will disagree. You either end up with crossed wires or discussions that take four weeks instead of one day.

The two owners were almost night and day. One of them was Anderson, a CEO for a Fortune 500 company. He presided over 35,000 employees, and was accustomed to hiring people to do jobs that he had no experience or interest in. He was smart as a whip but also knew that captaining a boat was my job, and he deferred to my experience. The kind of guy I could easily work with.

The other owner was another story. Harry was a California attorney, specializing in lawsuits. Three red flags right off the bat: lawyer, California, lawsuits. This was the kind of guy who was used to operating mostly on his own, without having to work with a team, and whose area of expertise was suing people for screwing up. He also had a pretty high opinion of himself. In other words, the perfect boss.

Having two bosses wasn't the only issue at play, however. Another problem was that they'd bought the boat half-finished. That's not a unique situation. Sometimes, a customer will put in an order and then suffer some financial reversals and not be able to take possession of the boat. The yacht builder stops work on the custom boat and looks to find another buyer. Enter Anderson and Harry.

Unfortunately, they didn't know what they were getting into. They bought the boat, but then hired some engineers who were just drooling at the chance to soak a couple of rich marks. They immediately started work on finishing the boat and started screwing things up.

I knew instantly that these guys had to go. For one thing, they'd installed the generators backward. That was, to use a very technical term, a big problem. As a result, you couldn't get access to service them, to check the fluid levels. On top of that, the plumbing and the wiring were all screwed up. My guess was that they put in a bid, got the job, then farmed it out to some bottom-of-the-barrel contractors to do the actual work. They got what they paid for.

Now, if you hire lousy contractors to renovate your home, you have some experience in living in a house. You can therefore call people on their shit when they do things like try to run the wires across the ceiling, or link pipes from the toilet directly to the shower. In those cases, you can say, "That just should not be," fire their asses, and get competent replacements. But virgin boat owners don't know what things should look like. When they came to visit the boat, they had no idea that the generators were installed backward. They were basically just looking at the hull, making sure there were no obvious breaches. They nodded their heads and said, "Let us know if you need more money."

That was, in part, why I was there. I knew what I was doing. When I saw the work that had been done, I wasn't happy. One morning, an engineer told me, "I'm going offsite to pick up some parts." Those parts must have been in Cuba, because he didn't come back for four hours and then just called it a day.

Another plumber was a total drunk, and if he got paid on a Monday, he was AWOL the rest of the week. That kind of thing didn't inspire a ton of confidence. I fired the whole lot of them and imported professionals who could get the job done. I had to rip out all the work they'd screwed up and redo it all from scratch. If you hire people who prove incompetent, you have to get rid of them.

Or so I thought.

Enter the chef. I'll call him Duane.

I was getting everything squared away on the boat for the Fort Lauderdale Boat Show. This was a big deal. We wanted to rent the boat out for charters, and it was the season, so we anticipated getting a lot of traffic from brokers interested in the boat. For that kind of thing, you want every piece of brass polished, every inch of teak on the deck scrubbed, and every member of the crew dressed smart, acting professional, and minding his manners.

Duane, our ship's chef, didn't get that memo.

"What's up, skipper?" he said as he walked up the gangway at six that morning.

"You Duane?" I asked. I hadn't met him before, but it was just process of elimination, since everyone had already showed up.

"That's what it says on my driver's license," he said, laughing at his own joke.

Who did he think he was talking to? The booking agent for the Ha-Ha Hut?

"You ready to work today?" I asked. The guy looked like he was in the final stretch of a three-day bender. Bloodshot eyes, unshaven face, not a lot of focus. Just the kind of guy I wanted cooking my food and swinging around razor-sharp knives.

"That's why they pay me the big bucks," he said.

A real charmer.

Problem was, I didn't have a lot of options. Just like I'd inherited the boat and had to get it into shape, I'd inherited the crew, as well. This was the first time I'd met him, and I didn't have time to fire him and replace him, since we were supposed to entertain the brokers all day. But just because I couldn't fire him didn't mean I had to make it easy for him.

"Just point me toward the galley, my good man," he said.

"I don't think so," I said.

"What's that?"

"You got a uniform in that bag? Chef's coat?"

"You know it."

"Well, find a nice hook to hang it on, because you're going to be doing a different job today."

"Bikini inspector?" He laughed, the perfect audience for himself.

"Gangway duty. Talk to Jeff, the deckhand, about getting a spare uniform. And put some shades on."

"So nice of you to think about my comfort."

"It's not for you, it's for anyone who comes within ten feet of you and doesn't want to have to see those Ebola eyeballs. Get some coffee down your throat, get sobered up, get a uniform, and be back here in ten minutes."

While Duane was downing a cup of java and getting presentable, I made a call to Harry to let him know that we were about to be one chef light.

"What's the story on this Duane guy? Seems like a total zero," I said.

"Yeah, he's colorful, all right," Harry said. Not quite the response I was expecting.

"Maybe a bit too colorful. I'm thinking of making a change."

"But you can't fire Duane! He's a genius in the galley! Just one of the most talented people I've ever met."

"He sure as hell isn't the smartest."

"Please, just give him a chance to show you what he can do. He's an artist. Like Michelangelo!"

"Well, if Michelangelo had given the same kind of lip to the Pope, he would have been looking for a new gig."

"I know he's an acquired taste, but trust me, he's worth it. You've got to keep him on."

"He'll have to be reprimanded if he gets out of line."

"Of course! Absolutely! Just a genius! Like Picasso with food!"

I hung up and shook my head. New owners. Maybe this chef got Harry laid back in the day. I would have really enjoyed giving Duane his walking papers, but I was willing to give him another chance. That said, he was sure as hell going to be on a short leash.

It relieved me a bit to see him standing at the gangway, as I'd instructed. He was dressed in a uniform, a shit-eating grin on his face.

"What do you think, Cap?" he asked, giving me a twirl. "Does this uniform make me look beautiful?"

"It makes you look slightly professional, which is a big upgrade," I said.

"What do you want me to do? Press the flesh? Network with some billionaires?"

"See that patch of dock?" I asked, pointing to the area directly in front of the gangway.

"Yep."

"Stand on it. Make sure it doesn't fly up out of here."

"Come on," he said.

"Make sure nobody gets on the boat unless they're with a broker." Superyachts are cool. They're big, luxurious, opulent, and people want to see them. But if we permitted every Tom, Dick, and Harry onto the boat that wanted to take a gander but couldn't possibly pony up the 200K needed to book a charter, the crew would be busy all day showing off the boat to gawkers. Giving interested tourists a chance to look around was like giving a Ferrari test drive to any curious Joe with a driver's license. It was a good way to tie up the salesman and to risk damage to the asset. So, all I needed Duane to do was stand there and turn away the looky-loos.

"Uh, okay. How long's that going to be? It's pretty hot," he said, looking up at the sun, shading his hungover eyeballs with his hand, even with the shades there for protection. It was October, but October in Fort Lauderdale feels like July on Venus. It must have been 93 degrees with 95 percent humidity.

I turned my back on him and marched to the bridge. "Until I get tired," I said. Maybe I couldn't fire him, but I could work his hungover ass until he bled to death through those blood-shot eyeballs of his. Hey, he had his chance to make a good first impression, but I guess there's no dumbass vaccine.

After a couple hours, I went down to check on him.

"That section of dock fly off yet?" I asked.

"Right where you left it," Duane replied.

"Then you're doing a great job."

"Skipper, what do you think about giving me a breather? I've been here all day, and I'm melting out here."

It was true—the uniform shirt he was wearing was absolutely sweated through.

"That shirt looks pretty much done in," I said.

"That's for shit sure," Duane replied. "Glad you finally noticed."

Not the attitude adjustment that I'd been hoping for.

"Why don't you go find Jeff, the guy who loaned you the uniform."

"Got it. You want him to take the next shift?"

"Nope. I want you to get a clean uniform from him. That one's looking rough, and he's got a spare."

"Shouldn't this be his job?" he asked.

"Taking care of this boat is his job. Showing me you actually deserve to be here is your job."

Two hours later, he'd sweated through the new shirt, too. I made him stand there all day.

Unfortunately, I don't think he received the message I was sending.

The next big stop on our calendar was the Antigua Charter Yacht Show. It's one of the crown jewels of the charter world. Everyone who's anyone goes there. The docks were full of high-end yachts, but none of them was for sale—it was only for owners showing their boats for charter work. We were one of 135 boats in Antigua hoping to do some business.

And it was big business. A good yacht with a top-flight crew could easily fetch $200,000 for a single week of chartered cruising. If you found a month of steady work, you could make almost a million bucks. Brokers would visit the yachts to see which ones they wanted to promote. They were looking for mint-condition hardware and a crew who understood that "service industry" required a certain amount of service. In addition to competence in your job, those brokers were looking for good attitudes. Pleases and thank-yous. Service with a smile.

Not really ideal for someone like Duane.

The guy was aggressively rude. With everybody: captain, crew, clients, anyone he'd interact with. It's like he thought that there was a finite amount of respect in the world, and any time he gave it to someone, it would mean less for him, so he acted accordingly.

After our first day in Antigua, I asked our charter broker, Chloe, how things looked for bookings for the season.

"What's with your chef?" she asked.

"His problem is that he's kind of an asshole," I said.

"No kidding."

"What did he say to you?" I asked.

"It's like he went out of his way to try to turn me off. I asked him what his favorite kind of food to cook was, and he said, 'Delicious food, obviously.' I mean, what am I supposed to do with that?"

"I'm trying to find ways to keep him away from everyone but the chickens in the walk-in."

"Good strategy. It's going to be tough if he keeps this up. If he puts out that kind of attitude with clients, it's going to cut into business. Does he realize that charters pay for his salary?"

"I don't know if he realizes the earth is round."

"Can't replace him?" she asked.

"I think he's secretly married to one of the owners. Or has some kind of incriminating film on him. One of the guys loves him more than sliced bread."

"I'll try to work around him."

"You and me both," I said.

The thing with Duane was, even if you tried to avoid him, he still had a way of making his presence felt.

Every night, he liked to party. In the mornings, I'd be heading out at six thirty for my run, and that's when he'd be coming back to the boat, three sheets to the wind. And he wasn't coming back with the rest of the crew after a night of carousing. He'd be coming back alone after a night of doing something by himself. Nobody wanted to work with the guy, and nobody wanted to party with him, either.

One night in St. Thomas, Duane must have really redlined it, because he came back from his nightly debauch early for him, before sunrise. He went to his quarters, not too steadily, found his roommate's bunk, and puked all over it. Not content to confine his repulsiveness to one place, he then dragged his ass to the galley and puked all over that, too. Job well done, he managed to work his way back to his room, ignored the bed full of sick he'd delivered, and passed out on his bunk, which seemed to be the only thing onboard ship he hadn't vomited on.

I worried, or maybe even hoped, that his roommate would see what he'd done and kick his ass. God knows he'd be entitled. But his roommate, Nate, was Duane's polar opposite. He was from Honduras, and what he made on the boat in a month was more than most of his countrymen made in a year, so he was determined to keep the drama to a minimum and just work his ass off to make some bank. He held his nose, cleaned up the room, and somehow managed not to cave in his roommate's skull with a pipe wrench.

I wasn't quite so forgiving.

While Duane slept and Nate cleaned up his mess for him, I got on the horn with Harry, the owner so devoted to Duane's case, telling him what happened.

"The guy has got to go. He's a total disgrace."

"I know, I know, he's got some rough edges, but I'm telling you, he's worth it."

"I could replace him in under a day, and morale would improve dramatically." And the food might have gotten better, too. It wasn't like Duane was incompetent in the galley, but he wasn't extraordinary. He wasn't making up for his deficits as a human being with equal but opposite contributions at meal service. If he wasn't a great cook, and he wasn't a good crewmate, then why bend over backward for him?

"The guy is irreplaceable," Harry said. "Trust me."

It just made no sense. The only way Harry's plea was logical was if he was D. B. Cooper and Duane knew his true identity. Duane was like a bad flu that just hung around forever. Made you feel lousy, and just didn't let up.

"I think he has to go," I said.

"Let me talk to him. I'll make sure he doesn't do it again."

"You mean when he sobers up enough to be able to talk?" I asked.

"Yes, absolutely. Let me talk to him, and I'll explain it in a way that he can understand how important it is that he straighten up and fly right."

I gritted my teeth, but there wasn't much more I could do. The owner didn't want me to fire the guy, and unless I threatened to walk off the job, I didn't see how I could apply any additional leverage.

Owners can be a frisky bunch. When you've got enough money to buy a boat that requires a crew to work it, you've got more money than most people will ever see in a lifetime. And when you're that wealthy, there's a chance that you can lose some perspective.

Like not knowing how much a gallon of milk costs.

Or not understanding why people complain about lines and service at the airports, because you have your own Gulfstream jet.

Or blasting away with a shotgun in the middle of the ocean.

One time, I was working as the first mate on a delivery of a Huckins motor yacht, a nice 80-footer with an open bridge. It was the owner, the captain, the chef, and me, delivering the boat to Key West. Everyone seemed to know what they were doing, except the owner, Porter.

Porter was the kind of guy who seemed to think the world should cater to his every whim. It was the eighties, and cell phones weren't particularly common, but I had one. The reception was poor, and the thing was the size of a cinder block, but it connected me to the rest of the world, for a hefty per-minute fee. Porter seemed to think it was a pretty fun little gadget, and after checking on the boat's systems, I noticed him just sitting there, chatting on my phone, completely oblivious to the $3-a-minute charges he was racking up.

"Emergency call?" I asked.

"Just shooting the shit," he said, returning to his conversation.

He didn't seem to take the hint. And I would have loved to have ripped that phone out of his hands. He didn't ask permission to use it, and he didn't apologize for taking it without asking. He just talked for about a half hour before I finally suggested he wrap it up.

He hung up, angrily, and acted totally indignant that I'd want to exert some power over one of the things I'd bought and paid for. Because to Porter, *I* was bought and paid for. To his way of thinking, it was his money that allowed me to buy that phone in the first place and he had as much right to it as I did.

"You got calls to make? Because I thought you were supposed to be working," he said.

"It's about two hundred dollars per hour to talk on that phone."

"It's my boat." He said it like that was the answer to every question, the trump card that won every trick. *I'm the owner, I'm the one with the big wallet, I'm entitled to whatever I want.* Because he paid my salary it meant I owed him. If that meant he wanted to use my phone whenever he wanted, then that was just the cost of being on his payroll. Rules weren't big on his priority list.

Even when it was less about rules, and more about common sense.

Every day, Porter would sit down and play gin rummy with the chef. I imagine the chef liked playing cards with him about as much as I liked letting him use my phone. But it was hard to say no, even if it meant the chef would be playing cards right through lunch. All the while, Porter would be there, looking at his cards and drinking rum and Cokes. By two in the afternoon, he was totally plastered.

Maybe that's a good thing. Not good that he was drunk, but him being drunk was a hell of a lot better explanation for what he did next than him being stone cold sober and just thinking it was a good idea.

We were in Hawk Channel when we sailed through a school of flying fish. When spooked, those fish can really put on a show. They were only 8 to 10 inches long, but they still really caught the eye when they popped out of the water and glided 150 feet through the air. For me, the chef, and the captain, this was something beautiful and dynamic to appreciate.

Not Porter. For him, this was something he wanted to destroy.

He went down below and came up with a long box. Porter reached in that mystery box, pulled out a 12-gauge pump-action shotgun, and just started blasting away at that school of flying fish like he was shooting skeet.

"Damn, like shooting fish in a barrel, right? Right?" He just thought it was the funniest thing in the world.

What the hell was he thinking? The fish weren't giving us any trouble, so why start opening up on them with the shotgun? It wasn't part of some innovative fishing technique, since he'd just let the perforated bodies of the fish sink to the bottom of the ocean.

That wasn't the most objectionable part of it. He could have killed us! We were bobbing and weaving with the waves, the wind was blowing, and Porter was drunk as all hell. He could have lost his concentration or his balance or both and put a chest full of shot into one of the three of us. Or he could have missed us and blasted a hole in the boat or ignited some fuel. There was a long list of horrible things he could have done by taking out that shotgun, and none of them was balanced out by any kind of benefit. He just wanted to cause some destruction, and so he did.

Maybe I should have seen the writing on the wall when I first interviewed for the job. I came in with another captain I knew, both of us talking to the owner about his open positions, and we both got offers. My captain friend had a bit more experience than I did, and he declined the offer. Not sure if it was the money or something Porter said during the interview, or something he didn't say, or just something that my friend was able to sniff out, but he didn't want to get on that boat. Usually, the smartest way to live through a catastrophe is just to avoid it altogether.

I wondered why Porter even had the shotgun on board to begin with. Most places, when you arrived at port, you had to declare if you have any kind of weapons on board. If so, you had to give them up until you left. Or, you could just declare nothing, but if you got caught, then you risked losing the boat to impound or permanent seizure, and you risked getting the captain thrown in jail. It wouldn't matter if the captain wasn't the one with the gun or that the owner on board was the one calling the shots. What mattered, in terms of the law, was that if something illegal happened onboard the boat, it was the captain's responsibility. If the third officer is on watch when an oil tanker runs aground, the captain goes to jail. A mate drags the anchor through a protected coral reef in Belize? The captain goes to jail. So not only could Porter have killed one or all of us, but he could have got the captain some jail time. He just didn't give a shit.

That was just something I couldn't put up with. The guy was angry, drunk, and maybe crazy, and I didn't want to be anywhere near him when things really went south. I told the captain that I was done with it, and to drop me off at the next port.

"You serious?" he asked.

"As a heart attack," I said.

"I'd try to talk you out of it, but you're just making too much sense."

I got off on Islamorada, just southwest of Key Largo. I called my wife and told her she was going to have to drive south pretty much until she ran out of road to pick me up. I was just glad the check they gave me at the start of the cruise still cleared.

It was the first and only time I'd ever jumped ship. It's important that a man hold to his promises, but once the shotguns come out, those commitments are null and void. I'm not running the risk of taking a shotgun blast to the face just because the owner thinks it's hilarious to kill fish with a firearm. An owner who doesn't know what he's doing can be one of the most dangerous things on a boat.

An owner with a shotgun can kill everyone on board. An owner who hires the wrong people and won't listen to professionals can sure as hell kill morale.

In some ways, the US Virgin Islands (USVI) isn't a lot different from Antigua. Beautiful blue water, clear skies, warm weather, umbrellas in the drinks. There were a lot of constants in the Caribbean. Unfortunately, another one of the constants was Duane acting like a complete head case. It was like he thought he was some kind of misunderstood artist, an *enfant terrible*, like he thought he was to cooking what Pollock was to painting or what Marlon Brando was to acting or what John McEnroe was to tennis, except that this guy's food would never get through the first round of Wimbledon.

He just loved rubbing people the wrong way. He'd run into a deckhand in the middle of a passageway, and there was no way he was going to let him go by.

"Step aside, flunky," he said.

"What was that?"

"You heard me, cupcake. Make way for the big dog."

Then he pushed by. The arrogance on the guy was through the roof, even though there was nothing to justify it. How he didn't get his ass beat on a regular basis when he went out is beyond me. Usually, everyone just avoided him, and he became a pariah. Sometimes, though, there was just no getting out of his way.

It was the end of a charter, and as is tradition at the end of a voyage, the clients had invited the crew out for dinner and a couple of drinks. Everyone, including Duane, who wasn't typically all that social, agreed. He may not have been the friendliest crewmate, but he was never going to pass on free drinks, even if "a couple" wasn't really a quantity of alcohol he had any kind of familiarity with. He was the kind of guy who wouldn't stop drinking until he saw the bottom of the bottle.

Dinner had gone about as well as could be expected with someone like Duane at the table. Everyone was coming back on the little transport dingy when he just couldn't hold himself back anymore. After two hours of not acting like a complete asshole, he just had to vent some of his inner heel or he was going to explode.

For some reason, he targeted the chief stewardess, getting right in her airspace, and there was no escape for her. Seeing he had a captive audience, he started shaking his crotch right in her face. I don't know why he'd act that way, but he seemed to think he was God's gift to women. No self-awareness at all. His arrogance was off the charts, but he had nothing to be arrogant about. The guy had a unibrow that was pure prophylactic. He couldn't get laid in a women's prison with a handful of pardons. But he wasn't attacking the chief stew because he was trying to put the moves on her—he was just being an asshole because he was an asshole, and that was just the way he'd decided to show his colors that day.

She tried to make the best of it, tried to be professional in front of clients, but she couldn't let it slide. Desperate, she grabbed a fresh water hose and sprayed him a little bit, just to make it clear she wasn't finding it funny. He totally overreacted to getting a little water on him. He still had a take-home beer with him, and he poured it right over her head, right in front of everyone. Then he said, "Now who's wet, bitch?"

It was horrible. It was humiliating for the chief stew, it was unprofessional, and it was in no way something that anyone would expect or accept. The clients were mortified. They insisted that he apologize to her.

"Who? That bitch?" he asked.

They were not amused. They again demanded he apologize.

"She's not really bothered, trust me. She just sprayed me, and is acting all hurt now, just to get attention from the rest of you dummies."

Again, they made it clear an apology was mandatory.

Duane dropped to his knees, lowering his head in mock penitence.

"Please, I beg of you," he said, each word dripping with insincerity and sarcasm, "you've got to see how sorry I am! Oh, heavens above, accept my, like, super apology! For shame, for shame!" When he was done, he jumped up and said, "Not really, bitch."

When the clients told me what happened, I was livid.

"I want you to apologize to her, right now," I said.

"I already did that."

"I don't mean your bullshit song and dance."

"I think she liked it. She was totally into it. Most women are."

"I'm done with you."

"Fine, skip, I'll see you tomorrow for breakfast."

"No, I'm done with your shit. Go to your quarters and stay there until I hand you a plane ticket home."

"You're firing me?"

"No, I'm sending you to your room. When I get off the phone, then I'll fire you. There's no way we're working together after the shit you pulled."

"Okay, call Harry. And you might just be right. But don't be surprised if you're the one hitting the bricks, pops."

He talked a big game, but he did exactly as I'd told him, going straight to his quarters. Then again, where was he going to go? He was so drunk, he'd have been unable to find his way off the boat on his own. I wanted to kick his ass, but I also didn't want there to be any reason that he could give to Harry that might make him want to keep Duane around, or to suspect that I'd acted unprofessionally. He was my next call.

"Duane has got to go."

"What happened?"

I told him about how Duane treated the chief stew, and that it all happened in front of clients.

"That's pretty serious," Harry said.

"You got that right."

"I'll talk to him."

"I don't think so," I said.

"How's that?" he asked.

"Talking doesn't work on this guy. I've tried, you've tried, and he's still an asshole. There comes a point where all the promises don't mean anything. He is who he is, and it's never going to change."

"You're not giving him enough of a chance," Harry said.

"The guy's had more lives on this boat than a cat. I can't work with him anymore. Everyone on board, including the clients, hates his guts. I've got to cut him loose."

"You might be overreacting."

"Look, I'm at the end of my rope. He's an embarrassment to the boat and a damn lawsuit waiting to happen for you. I absolutely refuse to work with this guy. So, either you can let me fire him, or I walk, and you can find someone who actually can stand him. It's him or me. Just decide who's more important to you."

"Look, I don't think that's necessary."

"It was probably necessary eight months ago when I first came on board. Now it's just a fact. Do you want to find a new chef or a new captain?"

He thought for a few seconds, and I could tell there was an equal likelihood of him going either way.

"Obviously, a captain is more important than a chef," he said. Which was true, though he wasn't really answering who he'd rather have remain on the boat. "If you feel you have to let him go, then that's your call."

"Great," I said, and hung up.

By the next morning, I had a gift for Duane: a plane ticket taking him back to Florida, one-way.

"This was a piece of shit boat anyway," he said, taking the ticket.

"And the plastic," I said. As the chef, Duane had a boat credit card, for purchasing food, booze, scouring pads, and anything else he'd need in the kitchen.

"Yeah, sure, whatever," he said, handing it to me. "See you around."

"Let's hope not," I said. I was relieved that I hadn't been forced to use a crowbar to separate Duane from the boat credit card.

Turned out, that feeling of relief was a little premature.

There's a saying among mobsters, that if you're not stealing a little, then you're stealing a lot. And Duane not putting up a fight about the boat credit card should have told me that he had bigger plans for that line of credit.

Turned out that he'd had a duplicate made of the card, and as soon as he walked off that gangplank, he went directly to one of the nicest hotels in the USVI and got himself a $500-per-night suite. And he didn't confine his spending to the room. He managed to do a pretty good job of racking up charges for fancy restaurants, bars, and any other way he could find to entertain himself at the owners' expense. Even worse to me, as it turns out, is the fact that Harry was probably 100 percent okay with this.

I'd had it. Even though the owners had finally let me give Duane the boot, it was just outrageous that he'd lasted as long as he had. There was no excuse for it. The captain has to be the captain. He's the one that makes the tough calls, and if they want to second guess the captain, then they should get their asses down to the boat and make those decisions themselves. Just not the kind of arrangement I was looking for. As soon as I finished up the charter season, I told them I wouldn't be coming back.

And Duane? As soon as I was gone, that was the first person Harry called up. Wanted him back on the payroll. Even after showing up drunk. Even after pouring a beer on a crewmate and calling her a bitch in front of charter clients. Even after stealing from him to the tune of thousands of dollars by ripping off the boat credit card, Harry still couldn't see that Duane was bad news.

It takes a lifetime of blood, sweat, and tears to become a captain, but the only thing you need to be an owner is deep pockets. Some are good, and some keep hiring guys like Duane.

Live and learn.

Chapter 10

~~~~~~~~~

This Is Not Your Personal Fucking Party Palace

They say money can't buy happiness. And while it's true that poverty sure as hell can't get you much, there's no guarantee that having a ton of cash is going to make anyone's life a joy to live. When you live and work in the world of super-yachts, you see a lot of money. You need to be incredibly wealthy in order to inhabit that world. But that kind of money only gets you a boat—it doesn't buy you satisfaction, or peace of mind, and it sure as hell is no guarantee for happiness. There's a difference between buying a boat because you love the sea and buying a boat because you love to be seen. If you buy a yacht because you get a thrill out of being on the water, of being able to see the sunset over the horizon, of knowing you can go places and see things that most of the world is denied, then that vessel will be an instrument to open your eyes and touch your soul. If you buy a yacht because it's the best way to show the world your bank balance, then it's going to take you a little longer to reach nirvana.

My best experiences as a captain came with working with old-money owners. Often, these owners were taught to love the water by their father or grandfather, were taught that yachting was a way to experience joy. These owners were also taught that the people who worked for them were to be treated like people, like they had emotions and dignity, and in some cases, they were even taught to treat the people who worked for them like family. They would keep the same people on for season after season, for year after year. Sometimes, captains and crew would work the same boat, or a series of boats, for the same owner until they retired.

Not everyone worked that way, unfortunately.

New-money owners didn't perceive the people who worked for them in the same way. They saw their captains and crew as basically objects that did their bidding and could be replaced instantly should the need arise. The purpose of the boat was to advertise how successful they were, and the people who worked for them were supposed to contribute to that image. For a lot of those new-money type of owners, their money proved that they were special people. Their net worth was a way to measure how valuable they were as individuals. And when you think being rich makes you better, then it's perhaps not surprising, though at the same time horribly sad, that you might think that having to work for a living in order to pay the rent makes you worse. Those people would then, inevitably, treat people accordingly.

That was the kind of experience I had working with a couple I'll call Pete and Patty Monarch.

The Monarchs were so wealthy, they didn't just own one yacht, but two of them, a 120-foot Trinity called the *Sea Hag III* and a 116-foot Feadship called the *Sea Hag II*. I served as the captain of the Feadship, the "little" boat, which basically functioned as the supply ship and overflow hotel for the larger Trinity, which the Monarchs used as their flagship yacht for entertaining.

And did they entertain.

For winter, the Monarchs would keep their boats in San Diego, but when the weather got warm, and cravings turned from ceviche to pinot grigio, they would cruise them up to the Bay Area. They owned an enormous apartment just across the street from the water in a brand-new building, a palatial set of rooms that must have cost $25 million.

When I arrived with my crew, we docked right next to the *Sea Hag III*, and it looked like we'd caught them in the middle of some kind of fire drill. Everyone was running around, moving like crazy. What was the rush? They had just arrived a short time before we did. They'd docked purely for the purpose of cleaning up before the next party. That meant the crew had to work their asses off traveling for almost four days, bring the boat in, clean it from top to bottom, and restock all their stores before departing on a dinner cruise at seven o' clock that night. They made it happen, and they left on time, only to return after seeing the Golden Gate Bridge, Alcatraz, Fisherman's Wharf, all the standard highlights, coming back to the dock at two in the morning.

Time for a rest, right?

Wrong.

Just a few minutes after everyone from the cruise disembarked, a fleet of black SUVs arrived, disgorging a platoon of new, fresh guests ready to party. They got on the boat, and off they went, returning to the docks at about eight in the morning.

That's a hell of a strain to put on a crew. Work them for over three days straight, then, on no rest, make them go nonstop for another twelve hours? Demanding a pace like that seemed downright sadistic. But when you see the people who work for you more as trained seals or robots that can't feel pain or fatigue, it made it a lot easier.

The Monarchs were an unusual couple. They did things their own way, which was their right, but they also did things in a way that seemed to minimize their happiness while simultaneously putting a strain on everyone around them.

For instance, they lived in that gigantic apartment, and had every convenience money could buy: the best Viking pro ovens, the elite Sub-Zero fridges, the top-of-the-line Wolf cooktops. But they refused to use them. The Monarchs said they didn't want their apartment to smell like food. Okay, not a problem, since San Francisco is one of the greatest food cities in the world, with outstanding restaurants showcasing the most celebrated chefs on the planet. So, what did they do? They called down to their boat, ordering their chef to prepare their dinners, which we were instructed to send on a dolly, across six lanes of traffic, to their apartment. Well, that was also within their rights as owners, and we employed a very talented and well-compensated chef who'd graduated from a top culinary academy who could grill, sear, barbecue, sous-vide, or flambé pretty much any kind of menu they could possibly request. So, what did they want?

Mac and cheese. Pizza rolls. Frozen deep-dish pizzas. Franks and beans. Borderline TV dinners. And don't get me wrong—

I enjoy a good plate of mac and cheese every once in a while. But when you have the means to have anything in the world, why deprive yourself of something great? Why employ a chef on a yacht to make you hot dogs? There's a whole world out there to see and touch and taste—so why go through it wearing dark shades and rubber gloves?

Still, it was their money, and if they wanted to buy an apartment and never use the kitchen so they could eat hot dogs prepared on their yacht, then that was their call. The part that really bothered me was how they treated people.

A lot of the time, my boat was just a floating hotel. For the most part, Pete and Patty Monarch would prefer to do cruises in their boat, the *Sea Hag III*, and just use the *Sea Hag II* as a crash pad for guests that didn't quite make the A-list for their boat. One of those people was Irving.

Irving was an executive at their company, though calling him that conjures forth images of stiff collars, straight ties, leather briefcases, and some aura of professionalism. Irving, unfortunately, conveyed none of that imagery himself. As far as I could tell, what he brought to the plate was convincing Patty and Pete that he thought they were geniuses, and he was therefore indispensable.

He'd been on the *Sea Hag III*, partying all night with the Monarchs, when he finally decided to call it quits and head back to his stateroom on my boat. He dragged his ass in around four thirty in the morning and passed out. It wasn't my job to judge, so that was fine. But then at eight, I got a call from Patty.

"How's Irving doing over there? Does he need anything?" she asked.

"Well, he went down a couple hours ago. Still resting, as far as I can tell."

"Do you have fresh bagels ready for him? He likes fresh bagels for his breakfast."

"No, Patty, not yet. I was about to head out to get some, but I don't think there's much of a rush. Irving didn't get in until a little before five this morning, so if today is like most of the other days he's been on our boat, I don't expect he'll rise until about two this afternoon at the earliest."

"Are you saying you don't have them on board yet?"

"Not yet, but they'll be ready for him once he gets up."

"I didn't ask when he was going to get up, I asked if there were fresh bagels ready for him."

"Well, no. But he's not going to be looking for breakfast for—"

"You need to stop fucking talking back to me! It's your job to take care of my guests! Not judge how they like to party! He likes fucking bagels, you fucking idiot! Can you understand that? Can you understand that some people like bagels? And some people like corn flakes? And some people like motherfucking steak and eggs for breakfast? You can understand that, can't you?" Needless to say, she had a mouth that I wouldn't eat with, and a very limited vocabulary, to say the least.

"Of course," I said, gritting my teeth.

"Well, he likes bagels. And how do you think bagels taste best? When they're fresh? Or when they're stale?"

"Fresher is always better," I said, edging ever closer to the brink of my patience with this Tuesday.

"Thank you, god dammit! I'm so relieved that you aren't going to argue with me anymore on whether fresh is better than stale!

Christ, it seems like it should be so easy! So, if he likes bagels for breakfast, why don't you have fresh bagels ready for his mother-fucking breakfast?"

"Patty, he doesn't take his 'breakfast' until the afternoon. So, I could get bagels now, but that would mean that they're just going to sit in the galley, getting stale, for the next six hours."

"What time is breakfast?"

"I'm sorry?"

"Yeah, you should fucking apologize, you asshole! But what time is breakfast?"

"For most people, it's between six and eight in the morning."

"Thank you! Again! You've proved my point! Breakfast, Lee, is served IN THE FUCKING MORNING! Why are you try-ing to tell me that breakfast is served after noon? Which would mean that breakfast would come AFTER LUNCH? Does break-fast come after lunch?" Her logic, or lack thereof, never ceased to amaze me.

"No, it does not."

"Exactly! So, stop arguing shit with me and send someone out to get some bagels for Irving so he won't have to wait ALL MOTHERFUCKING DAY for someone to get him his GOD-DAMN breakfast bagels when he wakes up! Fucking hell!"

The line went dead.

It was a waste of money, but they had plenty of money. It was a waste of time, but we had some time to waste, so I sent a stew to buy a bagel sampler. Plain, sesame, poppy seed, cinnamon raisin, salt, onion, everything, all the bagels. And in six hours, once that collection had hardened to the point that we could use them as skeet targets, I'd throw them all out and send the same stew to do the same errand. The client gets what the client wants, even if, truthfully, what the client really wanted was to yell at someone to make herself feel big and powerful.

Mission accomplished.

Part of being a captain is knowing that there's always another problem behind that first problem.

A few hours later, Patty took half my crew onto her boat. Not sure why. Her boat might have had a few of their regular people out from sickness, or it could be that she'd just fired a bunch of people and then needed to borrow from my boat to make up the difference. That was certainly possible. They'd fire people all the time, for any possible offense. A stew was smiling too much, so she seemed unprofessional, get rid of her. A stew wasn't smiling enough and seemed mean, get rid of her. The dinners are being served too hot, get rid of the cook. The dinners are being served too cold, get a new cook. They really loved to flex their muscles and show people who had the power. Just something they got off on. It was a real problem, for a number of reasons.

Most qualified crew were provided by a management agency that specialized in employment for people working on boats. But the company didn't get their fee unless the person they staffed was able to last in the job at least ninety days. Problem was, Patty fired people so often, or drove them off the boat in tears, that nobody could last very long. This presented lots of headaches, in part because it meant that nobody on her boat was ever very experienced. They didn't know the boat, and they didn't know their crewmates, because they were being constantly replaced. Another problem was that the employment agency never got its money because nobody ever lasted three entire months.

Consequently, the agency stopped sending people to staff Patty's boats. This was less of a problem for me because my people didn't quit every five minutes. But it meant that Patty was forced to hire her crew from craigslist, literally, where the only thing they would have in terms of qualifications was "a loyal viewer of *The Love Boat*." A consequence of these pretty questionable hiring practices, in this case, was that Patty wanted to go on a cruise, and didn't have enough people, so she took from my crew.

Okay, fine. I wasn't planning on taking the boat out.

Until her son showed up.

Brad was Pete's son from his first marriage, in his early twenties, and Patty didn't like him one bit. Patty treated him like a proverbial redheaded stepchild, just couldn't stand that this was a living reminder that Pete was once married to someone else. You'd think that that might automatically create some kind of bond between Brad and me, that he would see how Patty treated everyone who worked for her and feel some kind of sympathy, some kind of shared traumatic experience that would make him view me, and all the crew, as like-minded allies, all in this together.

Nope.

Brad was spoiled. Like a lot of kids of the super-rich, he had learned that for parents with pretty much limitless resources, it was easier for them to just give him whatever he wanted rather than to ever instill discipline. It didn't have to be that way. Warren Buffett, the financial wizard who became known as the "Oracle of Omaha," once described how he planned on giving most of his billions to philanthropic efforts rather than to his children. He wanted to give his kids just enough so that they had "enough money so they would feel they could do anything, but not so much that they could do nothing." Brad had decided to take all the money in the world and become . . . a rapper.

Though Brad received almost no love from his stepmother, Patty's biological child, Sue, seemed to fare just slightly better. Sue was only sixteen and seemed like a pretty good kid, all things considered. Still, that genetic bond didn't guarantee Sue any more substantial access to good parenting. She was dating a guy at least a decade older than her, and her parents didn't seem to find anything to object to in their union. In my book, a guy who's in his late twenties dating a teenager isn't just a creep—he's a pedophile. Where does a guy like that even meet a teenager?

This didn't mean that Sue was ignored or forgotten. The Monarchs wanted to make sure that their daughter received plenty of attention. When she turned sixteen, they bought her a Lamborghini previously owned by Jaden Smith. Because if there's one thing a teenager needs to get her to movies, dates, and parties, it's a $300,000 car. While the time and attention her parents gave Sue were pretty minimal, they made sure that they spared no expense for other people to spend time with her. Their personal assistant told me, in what was either a brag or a confession, that Sue's parents would pay A-list celebrities to talk to her, to the tune of $25,000 per hour. Come grab a pizza with my kid and I'll give you a cool 50K. Nice work if you can get it.

It was the kind of attention that her half brother Brad never received. Maybe that's why he was so unpleasant. Or it could have been merely his exposure to additional years of his parents.

"Captain Lee, I want to take the boat out," Brad said. "My friends are coming by in half an hour or so, so have everything ready to go by then."

For a variety of reasons, this did not exactly get my toe tapping. Not only did I not have enough crew to take out the boat, but Brad wasn't always the easiest boss to work for. He'd done this in the past, where he would get $500 in sushi from the local market, then he and his friends would eat it while taking breaks to have sex with each other all over the boat. Since it was his family's boat, he didn't see the need to be discreet, and would use the public spaces like they would the most private of bedrooms. It's true that it was his parents' boat, but it was also a workplace, and it was not his personal fucking party palace. While a bit shocking, the personality behind the display shouldn't have been all that surprising—this was a person who thought the rest of the world should either satisfy his needs or remain invisible.

"Sorry, Brad, I just can't do it," I said.

"Excuse me?" he asked. He didn't have a hearing problem—just an attitude problem.

"I don't have the crew I need. Your mother—"

"Stepmother," he corrected.

"Right, your stepmother took my first mate and my engineer, among others. The insurance company requires that we operate the boat with a full crew. Without those people, we could get in an accident, and if we did, the insurance would probably refuse to pay for it—"

"I don't care about that stuff. I want to take the boat out, so make it happen."

"Well, I *do* care about that stuff. I'm the captain. I'm not going to put my crew, or you and your friends, in harm's way just because you don't think it will be that hard." What did he know about operating a mega-yacht? From Brad's perspective, we just pushed a big, red button marked "Go" on a giant console on the bridge at the beginning of a cruise, and then a second button marked "Dock" at the end of it, and that's how it all worked. Plus, someone brought him his food. A two-person operation at the most.

"I'm going to tell my mom," he threatened.

"Stepmom," I corrected. Before steam shot out of his ears, I continued. "You can call her up, but I just can't risk getting in an accident with half a crew. If you want someone to do that, you'll have to find another captain."

"Maybe we will," he said, and stalked off.

It wasn't long before the phone rang.

"You get over here. As in *right now*," Patty told me.

I knew it was going to happen. Brad hadn't been raised to develop any kind of social skills, so when told that he wouldn't be permitted to do something he wanted to do, his only choices were to 1) whine about it, or 2) tell Mommy and Daddy. So, after exhausting the first strategy without adequate remedy, he'd bravely embarked on the second as a last resort.

Even though Patty had taken half my crew hours ago, they were still tied to the dock. When you have a volatile temper but marginal organizational skills, you end up with lots of hurry-up-and-wait. I guess it was just good news that I wouldn't have to take a dingy all the way to Alcatraz to catch up with them.

As I walked from my boat to the *Sea Hag III*, I looked toward the apartment that Patty and Pete owned. I knew from visits to the apartment in the past that Pete liked to keep a high-powered telescope trained on his boats when he was there. It was kind of creepy. Here was a guy with billions of dollars, where you'd think that his time would be incredibly valuable, and he was spending hours every day just spying *on his own boats.*

Why? It couldn't have given him much of a voyeuristic thrill, since there wasn't a ton he was going to be able to see, other than crew polishing the brass or the occasional sunbather getting a tan. It couldn't have been as a security measure, since nobody was going to be stealing the boats. One theory I had was that Pete was determined to identify any visible crew, because they had a rule in their San Diego home that the help should *not* be seen by the guests. Crew could not be outside of the boat, on deck, or aft of the wheelhouse. They had to stand where they couldn't be seen by any of the guests or anybody in the house. Maybe Pete was keeping an eye on the boats to make sure that the hired hands stayed below or else would face a severe reckoning. It would certainly be consistent with their philosophy that their employees shouldn't even breathe the same air as the masters of the house.

Though it could have been something else. Maybe he was just the kind of guy who loved looking at his own expensive possessions? Or maybe he got some kind of perverse thrill thinking he was looking at us when we didn't know it. And it was precisely for that reason that I would always give a little wave to the apartment when I'd be visible to that lens, just a little *I know where you are, and I know what you're doing* to throw a little cold water on his god complex.

At the same time, it was preferable to be experiencing Pete's attentions from hundreds of yards away instead of face-to-face. When he was on-site for one of his marathon parties, the crew would run and hide from him like he had Ebola. If he found someone who wasn't already engaged, which from his perspective meant someone who wasn't performing a quadruple bypass (but which *would* include the patient undergoing the procedure), Pete would just talk his ear off. And I don't mean to say that he would have a long conversation with them. There was absolutely no back-and-forth going on between Pete and anyone who was stuck listening to him. It was just a volcano of verbiage from Pete. He was wound up like an eight-day clock.

"Did you see the Raiders game the other night? Great game! Well, not that great. I mean, Hostetler is no Ken Stabler, right? And Tim Brown was an amazing receiver. Just otherworldly. Like a super man. *Superman* was a great movie. Christopher Reeve played Super-man. And George Reeves played Superman in the TV show from the fifties! Reeves and Reeve! Coincidence? I doubt it! There are no coincidences. I think that Einstein said that. Great scientist. A Ger-man, too. Which Hitler wasn't. Everyone thinks that because he was the head of Germany that Hitler was German, but he was born in Austria, and a lot of people don't know that. But I know that, because I read a lot of books, like this one I read the other day . . ."

And that was just Pete's opening salvo. He would go on like that for literally an hour. It would be impossible for a member of the crew to disengage from it because they didn't want to be rude and they didn't want to be fired. Rather than figure out how to pull a Houdini-like escape from one of Pete's yarns, the crew would just try to run away when they saw him coming, scattering like roaches. There was just no stopping the guy. He wasn't always that wired, but when he was partying, I have to imagine that he had some kind of pharmaceutical assistance, a little booger sugar to help keep the lights on during one of his seventy-two-hour boogie sessions.

Patty, on the other hand, had a different method of communication.

"What's this I hear about you telling Brad that he's not allowed to use the boat?"

"I didn't tell Brad that he couldn't use the boat. I told him that nobody could use the boat."

"Are you saying my son is *nobody*?"

It was hilarious that Patty chose this moment to emphasize her relationship with Brad, even though most of the time, she took every opportunity to remind the guy that he was trash. The enemy of my enemy is my friend, I suppose.

"I just told him that—"

"No! You don't tell him ANYTHING! You're the help—you do as you're told. Understand?"

"I'd be happy to take him for a cruise, if you'd just let my engineer and first mate come back to my boat."

"They're not your fucking crew—they're mine. And it's not your boat—it's fucking MINE! You take our damn orders and drive the boat. You're a water chauffeur, got it?"

"Oh, I understand."

"If you fucking understood, then you wouldn't be saying no to my son. We pay you to follow our orders. *No* is not I word I ever want to hear from your piece-of-shit mouth. I want to make sure that something like this will never happen again."

"Trust me," I said, "*this will never, ever happen again.*"

Patty nodded, very pleased with herself, turned her head, and started drinking from her vodka and cranberry and vodka. She seemed to have heard "Yes, ma'am." I don't think she really heard what I was saying, which was "Take this job and shove it."

When I returned to the boat, Marcy, one of the stews, ran up to me in a bit of a state.

"What's wrong, Marcy?" I asked.

"It's, um, about one of the passengers," she said.

"Is everyone all right?"

"I think so. It's just, it's Irving."

"Is he finally up? Damn, I guess this means we need to send a runner to get some fresher bagels for him."

"Already done. But the thing is, when I went to his room to clean it, he'd left something that I'm not used to cleaning."

"Did he get sick?" I asked. Guys that age shouldn't burn the candles at both ends like he did—the body just wouldn't stand for it.

"He pooped in his shower."

"What?"

"Yeah, just left a giant, uh, dump in the shower, and I don't quite know how to handle it."

Jesus H. Christ—who takes a shit in the shower?! Either he couldn't control himself and just pinched one off while he was freshening up, or he knew exactly what he was doing and, I don't know . . . thought it was funny? Either way, he knew what he did, knew it was disgusting, and he still just left it for someone else to clean up.

"Marcy, don't worry about it. It's not your problem."

"I can clean it up, but I just . . . did I do something wrong that he's trying to send a message? Is this some kind of punishment?"

"No, not at all. How long have you been working this boat?"

"Just finished my first month."

"Hey, way to go. It's probably something you haven't seen a lot. I've been here two and a half months, and it's something you just get used to. But damn—you sure as hell shouldn't have to."

"It was kind of a shock."

"I'll bet it was. Marcy, just don't worry about it. I'll take care of it."

She was grateful, and I went to investigate the offense. Just as she had described, Irving had left a huge dump in the shower. He was just waiting for someone to literally clean up his shit. I guess Marcy should have been glad that he didn't insist she wipe his ass, to boot. I took out my phone and took a picture, then sent it to Pete and Patty.

"Really?" I said. It may not have been professional, but it was the perfect way for me to let them know how the guests looked at the crew, and how we looked at the owners.

I wasn't going to take Brad's orders.

I wasn't going to clean up someone else's shit.

At least Patty got her way, in a sense.

Me saying no was never going to happen again, because I was *gone*.

At sea, there are storms one minute, then clear skies and glass-like water the next. You can be in the engine room, wrestling with a latch that won't budge, but when you add just a fraction of an ounce more pressure, it gives way, never a problem again. And it can be that way with owners as well—you can go from a disaster to a real dream like lightning. I've had insecure bosses, ignorant bosses, drunk bosses, and bosses that stiffed me, but I've also worked for plenty of people who were smart, hardworking, and tremendously generous. You meet all kinds in this world, and it's not a surprise that the ones you'd work for would be pretty diverse as well. You hope for the best, and when you find a situation that doesn't measure up, you move on to one that might be better.

It didn't get much better than Angelo.

There's a laundry list of reasons why Angelo was such a great boss, but one of the biggest contributing factors may have been that he'd earned his money at sea. Before becoming a billionaire, he was a captain himself. He'd worked hard, showed a lot of ambition, made smart moves with his money, and he eventually became fabulously wealthy.

With that kind of background, perhaps it wasn't a surprise that Angelo would be extremely grateful for what he had and appreciative of those who did the jobs he used to do. He didn't bark orders and jump down people's throats and swear up and down as part of some kind of profane incantation that he hoped would get the job done. For Angelo, it was always a request.

"If it's not too much trouble . . ."

"If it wouldn't be a lot of work . . ."

"If you have the time . . ."

Angelo had hired his captain and crew for a reason—because we knew how to do our jobs. We wanted to perform well and safely, and he never forgot that. As a result, he knew that if he were to make a request, we'd do whatever was in our power to make that happen. If, for some reason, we envisioned trouble, he knew we'd be able to provide a good reason. He wasn't a doormat—everyone respected what he'd done and where he'd been. But not every action had to be some kind of contest of wills. Some owners needed to scream at their crew so they'd feel powerful, but Angelo knew he was powerful and successful. He didn't need to perform some kind of verbal assault kabuki to drive that point home.

Angelo didn't give orders, he made requests. And his latest request was one that would be impossible to refuse.

"My father-in-law just had back surgery, and is recovering in Baltimore, at Johns Hopkins. We chose the hospital because the surgical staff was so talented, but he doesn't know anybody in Baltimore. Would you consider taking the boat to Baltimore so he could share Christmas and New Year's with his family?"

I always wanted to be as helpful as possible to Angelo, but both he and I knew this wasn't the easiest request. It was November, and the weather was already worsening, getting colder and stormier. The Atlantic coast in December and January is no cakewalk. The temperatures would be below freezing, the waves would be big and angry, and there was a good chance of getting hit by a storm.

A good captain can deal with weather. There are two kinds of trouble you can get into: bad luck and getting caught. There are storms in the Mediterranean called mistrals that just hit you out of nowhere. These things will come whipping through the Med, totally unpredictable. The most you'll get is a two-hour warning before you get hammered by 70-knot winds and 15-foot seas, and that's some bad luck for the captain.

Bad luck is just what it sounds like—you do everything you can to be safe, but you still get smashed by a rogue wave or a nuclear sub surfacing under you out of the blue. Getting caught is different. Getting caught is when you know the situation is going to be rough, and you still go out in it, thinking that your varsity seamanship will overcome any obstacle. One is an issue of unknowns; the other is an issue of stupidity. There's a big difference between the two, and the man who can't recognize that will get people killed.

That's what happened to the *Andrea Gail*, the fishing boat whose destruction was recounted in Sebastian Junger's *The Perfect Storm*. That was a captain who took his boat out when everyone else was laying in the harbor, even though he knew it was hurricane season. Taking a boat out in winter in the middle of the North Atlantic, you just *know* you're going to get your ass kicked. The storm came, the boat got caught, and six men died when they didn't have to.

The same tragedy visited the *El Faro*. The captain of that freighter left Jacksonville in September 2015 knowing that there was a tropical storm close to where he was plotting his course. Meteorologists at the National Hurricane Center forecasted that the tropical storm would become a hurricane. That's exactly what happened, as Hurricane Joaquin increased in strength. The likelihood of encountering the storm seemed so high that one of the deck officers wrote an email bemoaning how "there is a hurricane out here and we are heading straight into it." The captain seemed to think it was worth the risk, and he pushed on. He had plenty of time to turn around, more than ample time to select a different route. But that's not the decision he made. He did not have to go into that storm, but he plunged in anyway. He got caught. As a result, thirty-three men died on the *El Faro*.

Being a captain is no joke. People's lives depend on you being able to do your job. Families depend on your intelligence and your experience to bring their loved ones home safe. A skilled captain isn't the one who "boldly" tackles storms like they're one of the labors of Hercules. A good skipper isn't the one who never says no to a job. A good captain is the guy who can accomplish his mission and keep everyone alive. You don't get extra points for degree of difficulty.

That said, a good captain should be able to navigate around difficult conditions given enough time to plan. We have access to the technology that allows us to get a pretty accurate idea of what weather conditions will look like ten days out. So, when Angelo came to me, he gave me enough time, maybe seven weeks, to make a plan for a safe travel window.

Not every owner is so wise.

Some guys love the rush of flying by the seat of their pants or shooting from the hip. They like springing things on their employees at the last minute because they think giving people lots of warning is coddling them. I knew a captain in Costa Rica whose owner had a real hard-on to see the Super Bowl, so he told his captain he had to go to the Atlantis Resort in time to make the game. The Super Bowl is in January, and traveling from the Caribbean to the Bahamas in the middle of winter is a real dicey proposition. The captain said he wouldn't recommend it, but the owner vetoed him, demanded he move the boat, said, "Just get it done. You can take off and leave or I'll have a new captain here in the morning who can take your place." So, he agreed. He got it done, all right.

They were looking at 12- to 15-foot seas, lousy conditions. There's a bell on the bow of a boat, with a clapper that just swings free. Nobody pulls a rope to make it ring—that bell only rings when the waves move the ship enough to roll the boat to the point where the clapper swings and strikes it on its own. When you hear that bell ring, you know you're in trouble. The bell was ringing on that voyage. The captain ran right into a storm that smashed up a new $75,000 tender, lost a Jet Ski, and rang up about 250K in damages to the boat. And no insurance company is going to pay a claim to a guy who ran his boat into a hurricane when every weather report told him not to just because he didn't want to miss the big game.

But even the captain would admit that what he did was stupid. Luckily, Angelo understood how the world and the ocean worked. He gave me enough time to plot a course and find a safe travel window. He also gave me a perfect reason to make the trip, something a lot more convincing than just screaming, "Get it done."

Angelo's father-in-law had bought the vessel we were going to be sailing, hoping that he and his wife would be able to use it as a retirement boat. Unfortunately, his wife had died before they set sail on their first trip, and Angelo's father-in-law lost all interest in the boat. When he injured his back, it made it impossible for him to travel comfortably, so we decided to bring the mountain to Moses. We would bring his kids and grandkids on the boat and make a special holiday reunion.

In order to make this happen, Angelo would do anything. He appreciated that it wasn't going to be an easy sail for me or my crew.

"Captain Lee, it will be cold, so I want you to buy foul-weather gear for all the crew. The best. Anything you need, you come to me."

Angelo really pulled out all the stops. One of our crew, an engineer, didn't want to be separated from his wife during the holidays, but she couldn't afford to take off work to accompany him on the trip. So, Angelo offered to hire her on to our boat for the entire trip, so they could be together and we wouldn't have to find a replacement engineer.

He was extremely generous. So much so that he'd been horribly abused by one of his previous captains. That guy just saw Angelo as a big, fat paycheck. He was already getting paid a very nice salary, but that wasn't enough for the guy. He would find ways of screwing over Angelo every chance he got.

One of his cons was the car scam. This guy had convinced Angelo that he would need a company car to run errands once every few weeks. Angelo agreed, offering him a travel budget of $1,000 a month for rental cars. So, this bastard bought himself a beater Camry for $2,000, and then would rent it to himself and bill Angelo $1,000 a month to drive his own car. A good way to add another $10,000 to your annual salary. And it didn't stop there.

At one point, the boat needed to get some more substantial work done, so Angelo told the captain to hire some day laborers to do the job. It would take a couple weeks to complete, but nothing too technically demanding. So, what did this guy do? He hired the workers but told them that he'd offer them affordable rates if they just slept on the boat, which he *charged them for*. He then docked their pay for the lodging, which he paid to himself. So, he ended up turning Angelo's boat into a hotel, screwing both the workers and his boss.

I don't understand why he needed such a complicated scam, since the ex-captain also resorted to straight-up robbery. After I'd come on, Angelo would call, asking if I needed more money in the safe for petty cash.

"Nope, I'm fine, Angelo," I said.

"Are you sure, Captain Lee? It's no trouble."

"No, we're doing fine with what we have. Thanks."

We didn't need a ton of cash. We weren't traveling. We'd resupply food and drink as demand required it, but it wasn't more than a couple thousand a month. After three months, Angelo called me, extremely anxious.

"Captain Lee, are you certain that you're not running out of cash?"

"Yeah, certain, Angelo. Why?"

"Well, the last captain just needed a lot more, like fifteen thousand dollars a month."

Ah—that was the problem. The captain was asking for "operating expenses" that went right into his pocket. Another $180,000 a year as part of his benefits package.

"Must have been for a leak, but that leak is fixed now," I said.

I wouldn't take advantage of Angelo, never. And he always looked after his own people like they were family. Before we set sail for Baltimore, he made it clear that he wanted us to be as safe as possible.

"Please, Captain Lee, stop every night. Take your time. Don't push too hard."

We did take our time, which in those conditions was mandatory. Everyone watching me leave the Port Everglades and hang a left to go north instead of south thought I was batshit crazy. But I wasn't crazy enough to rush. We actually took more time than we should have, but it wasn't because we were pacing ourselves.

At one point, we ran into a real spot of trouble. Going from where we were, in Florida, to Baltimore, would normally take about three days. We had the Gulf Stream current on our side, which goes south to north. We expected that to give us a 4- to 5-knot boost. But once we reached Cape Hatteras, the engines just died.

Problem.

We were bobbing like a cork in a washing machine, running into 6- to 9-foot waves. Shit's flying all over the place with no propulsion, no control. We bled all the injectors, but I was just dumbfounded. What the hell had killed the engines? The engineer had no idea. Something mechanical? Electrical? Something with the hydraulics? So far, we'd found nada. Not confident we'd be able to solve the problem before getting knocked around enough to break something even more important, I called the tugboats to come help us. We were 60 miles off shore in a shit sandwich—I wasn't too proud to ask for help. I was pissed off and covered in diesel fuel from poking around the engine room, so I went to my quarters to clean up and cool off. With no other great ideas, I hit the showers.

Sometimes, when you can't figure things out, it doesn't hurt to change your perspective.

I was standing in the shower, my leg braced against the bulkhead so that I didn't get flung around from the waves hitting us. My mind, just wandering on its own, started thinking of another vehicle that just died. It was in the movie *Beverly Hills Cop*, when Eddie Murphy disabled an unmarked police car by sticking a banana in the tailpipe. Pretty funny. The exhaust had nowhere to go, and eventually, it killed the engine.

Wait a minute—did we put a banana in our own tailpipe?

I ran out of the shower, naked as a jaybird, soap everywhere, and got on the horn to the engineer.

"Did you close the underwater exhausts?" I asked him.

"I thought I did," he said.

When you ask someone a yes/no question, and they respond, "I think so," they are really saying, "No, but don't quote me on it." That wasn't good enough, not for me.

"You get your ass to the engine and make sure they're closed," I told him.

Sure enough, that was the problem. We'd left open our underwater exhausts. With too much back pressure, we'd suffocated the engine. We switched to the side exhausts and the engines came roaring back to life.

Still, I didn't want to take any chances. I told the tugs to keep on coming just in case there was more to the problem than the exhausts, or in case we'd sustained more damage than I realized. And it's a good thing I did, too. Half a mile from shore, we got enveloped with fog thicker than cold oatmeal. Just nothing for visibility. This was a real problem when entering an incredibly narrow inlet with maybe 15 feet of clearance on each side. It took three tugs to get us the last 10 miles to the dock, one at the stern, one at the bow, and one running as a scout with all its lights on just so we could have something to follow.

We stayed there docked overnight, got everything cleaned up, and then headed to Baltimore. It was a pretty uneventful trip the rest of the way, not to say it was a pleasure cruise. The biggest shock was the weather.

That dock in Baltimore Harbor was *cold*. As soon as water would hit the boat, it would freeze solid. There was soot all over because of the diesels, to the point where it looked like we'd been sitting on top of a smokestack for a year, but we weren't going to be washing that off anytime soon, because to do so would encase us in a block of ice. The lines mooring us to the dock quickly sprouted six-inch icicles. Even though it was cold, it was a relief to get to where we'd wanted to go.

Angelo's father-in-law loved the trip. He was able to see his family and enjoy the boat for basically the first time. It also rescued him from the hospital. He still needed twenty-four-hour professional care while he was recovering from his back surgery, but Angelo had that figured out, too. He built a cabin for his father-in-law equipped with every device he'd need, as well as a berth for a nurse he hired to look after the man 24/7.

Once we finished, Angelo gave everyone two weeks' bonus pay for making the trip, which was a nice Christmas gift indeed. Before he left on his private jet, he insisted that I stop every night on the way back and that I take the crew out for every dinner.

"Please take them to a nice restaurant. I do not want the chef to have to cook for anything. I don't care how long it takes to get back. Take a week, take two weeks, I don't care. Take it nice and slow, take it easy, and make sure everybody rests up."

He really appreciated what we contributed, and he made us feel valued as part of the team.

If Angelo ever called and said he needed a captain, I'd be there in a heartbeat.

It cost about the same amount of money to buy the *Sea Hag III* as it did to buy Angelo's boat, but there was an ocean of difference between the two men who made those purchases. Just because you have a big bankroll doesn't mean that you're a genius. Just because you've got the cash to hire people doesn't make you a leader. Perhaps most important, having a lot of money doesn't automatically make you happy. The Monarchs had all the money in the world, but they weren't happy. Their family spent time together, but they seemed to resent every second of it. They were insecure, petty, undisciplined, superficial, and could only seem to take pleasure in cruelly exercising their power over others. Angelo was happy in great part because he was respected, and that's because he gave respect to others. He was happy because he loved his family, and they loved him in return. They didn't love him because he was rich. They loved him because he'd spent the time to raise them, he prized his time with them, and he showed great strength of character. He had worked hard to develop that character in his children and grandchildren.

I've worked for bad owners and good ones, and while it was never a joy to work for the bad ones, it sure allowed me to appreciate more fully how good I had it when working with people with class. Nothing comes easy in this world. If you want to be a good captain and cross stormy seas in winter, you need to take your time. Plan with exacting precision and surround yourself with good people. If you want to be a good man, do the same.

Chapter 11

Don't Embarrass Yourself or the Boat

I'd been working in the business for twenty-five years when I got an interesting call. The head of our charter management company wanted to tell me about a new opportunity.

At the time, I was working as the captain of a 50-meter Benetti, the *Cuor di Leone*. The owner actually had two boats, the Benetti and a 120-footer. Not typical, but the guy had money that kept his other money from getting lonely. We were working the charter show in Miami, and there was a new charter client potentially interested.

"Captain Lee, we've got some TV people interested in chartering the boat," said our agent at Charter Management.

"That right?" I said.

"Yep. The Bravo network is planning on doing a show about yachting. You ever hear about that?"

"Yeah, I think I heard something through the grapevine." A few months before, those of us in the yachting world had heard that a TV network was interested in casting a yachting show. They needed a captain, deckhands, stews, the whole works. They were asking people to submit applications, headshots, video screen tests, and that kind of thing, if they were interested in being a TV star.

My response, at the time, was no thanks. I already had a job. And why would anyone want my ugly mug on TV? I'd spent a lifetime at sea. My face had weathered things like sunlight and salt air. I didn't look like I spent half of every day in a spa, or half of every dollar for a plastic surgeon. My dream wasn't to be famous. My dream had always been to be a captain—to spend my life commanding vessels, going from one beautiful island to the next, and have a few umbrella drinks along the way. The only stars I was interested in were the kind I could navigate by 100 miles from the nearest city, when the clouds blew away and it was like looking into infinity.

Besides, I didn't have a clue how to make a video screen test, and I wasn't looking to expand that particular horizon.

"Well," the agent said, "it looks like they've cast their show, and now they need a boat to film it on. They're looking at a six-week charter down in St. Martin and St. Barts. Think you could give them a ride?"

"Do I have to do any on-camera bullshit? Or can I just do my job?"

"They've got a guy they hired as the captain. But he doesn't have any time on the boat, and you do, so I'd like you to be there, just in case. All you'd have to do is keep an eye on the boat."

"I think I'm qualified for that."

"And get paid."

"I'm *definitely* qualified for that."

"Great! Should be a pretty uncomplicated in-and-out."

But as I'd learned from my earliest trips with Crazy George, or when I had worked that simple sail that turned out to be a drug boat, uncomplicated jobs could be surprisingly complicated.

By the time I arrived, there was already a problem. Kevin, the guy that Bravo had hired to be the captain, was qualified to captain the boat. That is to say, he had a license that allowed him to sit behind the wheel of a 165-foot yacht. However, the insurance people weren't so sure about that. Yes, he had the proper license, but he just didn't have enough experience to make them comfortable enough to insure him.

One of the producers had an idea that he thought might solve all their problems.

"Lee, you're licensed for this boat, right?"

"It's one of the requirements of being the captain."

"And the insurance company insures it with you as captain?"

"Wouldn't be much point to hiring me if they didn't."

"Yeah, yeah, we're learning that. So, what about this: since you're here anyway, what if we have Kevin, our captain, be, like, the 'pretend' captain?"

Always be skeptical of a man giving you air quotes.

"What's a 'pretend' captain?" I asked.

"Well, you'd do all the captain stuff. You'd be the real captain. But any time that they need something, people would go to Kevin first, and pretend he was the captain, then they'd go to you, for the real stuff. Like, they'd put the camera on him to drive the boat, but you'd really be doing it from one of the wing stations. Things like that."

"So, they'd ask him questions about running the ship, for the cameras, and then they'd come to me to get the real orders?"

"Exactly."

"And you're making a *reality* show?"

"That's right."

"With a real ship and a fake captain?"

"More like a pretend captain. He's not an actor or anything. He's really a captain. He would just pretend to be the captain for this boat, when you're the real captain. Like a secret captain."

"And you'd pay me real money to be this secret captain?"

"Absolutely."

That was certainly intriguing. I was already getting paid by the owner to babysit the boat. Now I might be getting paid by the TV people to babysit the captain? They had my attention, but it just didn't seem kosher to me.

"So, I get paid twice to do one job? Sure, I can swing that." But I knew in reality that it wouldn't work. On any vessel, there can be only one captain. It's like the laws of physics that never change. As they said in the cult classic Sean Connery movie *Highlander*, there can be only one.

Here was the problem, a problem that pretty much no one involved could have possibly foreseen except me: as everyone who is in yachting knows, the captain is a pretty integral part of running a charter boat. Nothing, and I mean nothing, happens without him or her.

It just wouldn't work. If someone had a problem with the engines or the generators or the water stores or the crew, they'd have to come to the captain. The captain is the boss. You can't try to produce episodes of *Top Chef* with pretend chefs, you couldn't make *Project Runway* with pretend designers, and you can't make a reality show about a yacht with a pretend captain.

So that's how I got on the show. They needed a captain, and I happened to be the captain of the boat they planned on filming on. Package deal, I guess. Plus, it made things easier all the way around. I knew the boat, was already insured, and the owner already approved me. It just made a lot of issues into non-issues.

Even though I hadn't gone through the audition process, there were still a few hoops I had to jump through.

Hoop number one: they had to make sure I wasn't crazy.

Good luck with that.

These days, if you want to be on a reality TV show, you have to pass what's called a psychological evaluation. Because, and this came as a real shock, a lot of people who want to be on TV are total sociopaths who will do anything to get famous.

This need for psychological vetting got started back in the nineties, when tragedy hit *The Jenny Jones Show*. Jones was doing a show about secret crushes and managed to convince a man named Jonathan Schmitz to participate in the show, because someone had revealed that they had a secret crush on him. Schmitz agreed, believing that the crush was from a woman (as the show's staff had implied). He was shocked to discover that the person who had the crush was another man, Scott Amedure. Three days after the segment taped, Schmitz tracked down Amedure and shot him to death. He told the police that he'd murdered Amedure because he had humiliated him by putting him on the *Jenny Jones* show.

So now they make you pass a crazy test.

The problem for me was, I like to have a little fun. I've got an occasionally warped sense of humor, and this situation just seemed pregnant with comic potential.

"You nervous at all for your psych test?" one of the producers asked me.

"Not at all. Sounds like fun."

She must have seen the glint in my eye or heard something in the pitch of my voice, because she immediately said, "Don't screw it up."

I wasn't going to screw it up. But at the same time, wouldn't the person who evaluated cast members for this show enjoy a little something unusual? I mean, I wasn't going to bay at the moon, but at the same time, I thought that it might be funny if, during the evaluation, I started drooling out of the corner of my mouth or developing a twitch on my face. Or if I acted like I thought the first mate was a hat rack. You know, something subtle.

But I didn't want to get anyone in trouble for saying, "Let's give Captain Lee a chance to do this, because he's not a crazy person." I played it straight, managed to not get labeled too deviant, and moved on.

A second hoop I had to jump through was a pretty comprehensive background check. They just needed to make sure that I was who I said I was and that I didn't have any skeletons in the closet. Yet another time I was incredibly thankful that the drug boat I was unknowingly transporting was only filled with secret compartments and not floor-to-rafters weed.

Then I did a few Skype interviews to show them I was, if not telegenic, then at least capable of speaking in complete sentences. Relying on decades of experience and discipline, I again managed to not start barking like a dog. Finally, I was rated fit for television duty.

Now came the hard part.

I'd never worked with TV people before, and because of this inexperience, I ran into trouble on two levels: 1) not knowing exactly how to make something work effectively for TV, and 2) butting heads with the TV folks over who's in control.

The first problem wasn't entirely unexpected. TV people are used to either working in the familiar, controlled confines of a studio, or "on location," which still usually means "on dry land." If someone was shooting a reality show about truckers in Alaska, they still had some idea about how to mount cameras to cars and trucks, how to shoot footage in the cold, how to move from the interior of a building to the parking lot, that kind of thing. Unfortunately, we ran into a bit of a brick wall when it came to shooting at sea.

How do you do it? Well, you point the camera at things and then press Record, but even that skips over some important stuff. How do you get a camera crew ferried over from outside the boat to the inside? How do you put the camera in the water to take shots of the boat from the exterior perspective? What can you mount to a passageway if you want to attach a camera for a long tracking shot? Does salt air affect the equipment? How does shooting outside in the open air during day or night affect lighting? What's the best way of tracking a group moving at high speed on the water while water skiing or boogie boarding? These are things we had to figure out on the fly.

And speaking of flying, we also had to figure out how to fly.

One of the things that the producers loved was the scale. The ship is enormous, the horizon is infinite, the water is expansive—everything has an epic quality to it. So how do you capture that kind of immensity? One of the producers had the idea of filming with drones. Like many great sea stories, this one began with the phrase "It seemed like a good idea at the time."

Not only was the crew not fighter-jock elite at operating drones, but the hardware for the drones was still in its infancy. That said, a producer, Phil, still thought it would be a great way to get both a wide perspective on the exterior and also be able to add some kinetic movement as the drone moved either toward the ship or away from it. I can't deny that, in a perfect world, this would have been a great idea. You could get a shot that started hundreds of feet above the ship and then swept in toward the bridge. Or you could start with the camera focused on a single shot of the stern, and then pulled back to show the ship and also the horizon at sunset at St. Martin. It would have been beautiful.

In a perfect world.

Unfortunately, we live in a world where the captain of *El Faro* navigated his ship directly into a hurricane that he knew was right there. A world where the Monarch clan tortures employees for sport, where Alex felt totally comfortable hiring guys like me to sail his drug boat, the *Southern Nights*. It's imperfect. And so that drone went up . . . and then crashed right into the drink. On day *one*. We stopped trying to use drones at that point, and instead got helicopter flights for big exterior shots. Live and learn.

An important aspect of negotiating technical issues was communicating with TV people about the boat's capabilities.

For instance, they suggested that it would make for a good shot if we could get the (rechristened for TV) *Honor* to steam right up close to a beach. The problem was, that beach was just too shallow. We were drawing 10½ feet, and the beach was only about 8 feet deep. We can only go as shallow as the boat displaces the water. So, I had to veto the ship-on-the-sand proposal. This was nothing personal. They weren't being overly demanding or anything—they just didn't know the technical requirements for what boats could or couldn't do. In general, my approach was that if we could do what someone wanted safely, then we'd do it. If we couldn't, then we'd have to think of something else.

In addition to the technical learning curve, there was a personal learning curve as well. One of the big problems I encountered early on in my first season: people who wanted to be stars. On a boat, there's just one authority figure: the captain. He gives the orders, and everyone else follows them. He's not the captain because he likes drama. He's the man because he's earned the right to be the man. This was the root of my trials with Ashley.

Ashley had been hired as both the chief stew on the show and also some kind of technical consultant. Because of that title, she thought that she was the person who would be calling the shots. But she had no clue what it meant to be a chief stew, much less the commander of the whole boat. She seemed to have a god complex. But on a properly run boat, the only god on board is the captain.

"Look," Ashley said. "We're going to need a new kind of morning routine if it's going to be the way I want it."

"Oh really?" I asked. She was a legend in her own mind.

"I just need to make it in line with what I've seen on other boats I've worked on. And there are some things I'm going to need you to do."

I let her go on like that for a few more minutes before I beckoned her in my direction.

"Ashley, could you step into my office for a minute?" I asked.

She nodded, a smile on her face. I imagine she thought that I was going to ask her how to run the ship, or maybe that I was going to promote her. But that wasn't on my to-do list.

"Look, Ashley, I like that you're excited. But you can't be giving anybody the impression that you're the one in charge. I don't know who you think you are or what you think you're doing, but the only thing I need from you is to be the best chief stew that you can be. I'm not taking orders from you. Get that through your head right now. I just need you to keep your mouth shut and do your job. Keep it that simple, or we'll have a problem."

She left my office in tears.

I got a call from production shortly thereafter.

"What happened with you and Ashley?" a producer asked.

"Nothing. I just told her how it was going to be."

I think they were just mad they didn't get it on camera.

I didn't want to hurt her feelings, but at the same time, I'm responsible for all the lives on my boat, clients and crew. It's a responsibility that isn't going to vanish just because someone wants to be the big enchilada. I was happy to do the show, but running the boat would always come first.

~~~~~~

Our days started early. By six, I was exiting my quarters, fully mic'd up. That's just the way things worked on the boat. As soon as you got up, you got wired for sound, and that's how you stayed for the rest of the day.

It was a bit of a fishbowl. On a boat, even a luxury yacht, there's still a finite amount of space for everyone to operate. You'll be in fairly tight quarters with the same faces day in and day out. On top of that sense of claustrophobia was the realization that pretty much every inch of the ship was on *Candid Camera*. While there was a film crew always looking for the most interesting situation to capture on their cameras, there were stationary cameras throughout the ship. The only places that didn't have cameras were the guest rooms, the guest heads, and the captain's quarters. Every other inch of the ship was fair game.

There was a TV crew of fifty or so on the show. That was a lot considering that we had a pretty packed boat already, with a full crew and a full complement of charter guests. Once the day started, it was just business as usual. We'd try to make the guests happy, and whatever happened, happened.

Still, some people just wanted to be stars. Ashley was that way. I had an engineer, Skip, and he was that way, too. A real fame whore. One time, I thought I gave him a real straightforward assignment, but then things got complex.

"Skip, do me a favor and change the filters in the air handlers, would you?" I asked.

"Sure, Captain. I just need to find a camera and sound guy, and I'll get right to it."

Wrong answer. There were about fifty air handlers that he would need to locate and change their filters. It was enough work that I didn't want him to double his time by finding someone to document it properly.

"No," I said, "what you need to do is get your tools and get to work. If production wants to film you changing filters, I'll let them know where to find you. Now move it."

He sure as hell didn't like it, but he did it. He was the kind of guy who would always try to find a way to inject himself into a scene, but that's not what I wanted from my crew. It's not even what Bravo wanted from their show.

He really wanted to be on camera. And if there was one thing about television that I had learned at that point, it's that the average viewer wasn't always on the edge of their seat waiting for someone to change an air filter. Not sure why he thought that was must-see TV. The problem was, the kid had drunk the Kool-Aid. He knew there was a TV crew on board, and he thought that was his ticket to wealth and fame.

But what was his thought process? His end goal seemed to be that he wanted to be a big celebrity, like Julia Roberts or George Clooney. Is that how either of those stars began their careers? Exuding raw charisma while changing an air filter? Didn't Skip realize how desperate he looked? I guess not. He'd have a better chance of seeing God twice in one day than becoming a big celebrity.

The main thing I hoped he learned from that little exchange was that the camera crews worked around us. We made things happen through the course of our work, and they recorded it. It never worked in the reverse, where they would give us scripts and we would follow them. There was enough going on in my reality that I didn't need a writers' room adding new ideas.

That's just the way it is for a captain. Crises pop up, personalities clash, and that's just part of the job. Shit happens—sometimes literally.

One time, on another yacht I had command of, we had the owner's nephew, Johnny, on board, and Johnny was one first-class pain in the ass. He was just eleven years old or so, but he had the destructive ability of someone far more senior. I just wanted to boil that kid alive. Johnny's primary focus seemed to be the boat's toilets. Now, the plumbing onboard a yacht is pretty sensitive, so you can't be throwing too much down there. If you didn't eat it first, and if it's not marine-grade toilet paper, it doesn't go in the commode. Johnny, apparently, saw this as a challenge. He'd throw an entire roll of toilet paper down the head just to see what would happen, and it would clog everything up.

When that would happen, and it happened four or five times, I'd have to go down to the bilge and unclog it. It was a pretty disgusting duty, since I didn't know which of the collectors had the clog, so I'd have to go to every one and open it up, which meant draining a five-gallon container full of piss and shit. It wasn't a joy to look at, and it smelled a hell of lot worse than it looked. Once I found the right one, I'd unclog it and tell Johnny, for the fifth time, not to do it again.

So, I was down there, with my face right up against the inspection cap, trying to see if this one had the obstruction, and that's when Johnny decided to really get me—he flushed.

I got BLASTED. And I wasn't getting blasted with water—I was getting showered in some grade-A ship's sewage. It really gave new meaning to the term "shit-faced." I went to find the owner and said, "Go get Johnny, and bring him to me." I took Johnny by the collar down the bilge, where I showed him what he'd done, in Technicolor.

"Now if this happens one more time, you're going to eat this for dinner," I said. That seemed to finally put the fear of God into him. Just to be sure, I made him stay down there in the bilge until he was gagging.

It's a shame that happened before I was hired on to a reality show. That would have made pretty good TV.

Still, I had, on some level, a bit of admiration for the kid. Johnny was trouble, but he was smart, and he liked to mix it up. Part of the reason that he was hell on wheels was because he just didn't have enough to stimulate him on the boat, so he made his own fun. The kid was part pirate, and there was something in me that saw a kindred spirit.

Sometimes, of course, the camera was right there even when you had moments when you wish they weren't. Perhaps the most memorable one of those kinds of adventures was when we had some photographer clients who had brought what I suspected was cocaine onto the boat.

Lots of people seem to view yachting as some kind of above-the-law form of recreation. They think that going out into the ocean means that we're in international waters, and that laws no longer apply to them. That might mean that they can play all the high-stakes pai gow they want to, but it doesn't mean you can transport hard drugs. It looked like at least one of these guys was using the same logic as a seven-year-old who says he can do whatever he wants because "America is a free country." Sure, kid, that's how laws really work.

It was a tough situation to be in. On the one hand, we want clients to be happy. On the other hand, I don't want my boat to get boarded by the Coast Guard, and I don't want to go to jail for twenty-five years. I made the decision to kick them off the boat.

Making that decision wasn't the end of it. I knew that they'd be pissed, and I sure as hell didn't want anyone trying to get revenge on me, or the boat, by leaving some of their Brazilian marching powder behind and then making a call to the Coast Guard saying that we were smugglers. That would be petty as hell to do, but in my experience, people can be petty as hell, so you protect yourself. I assigned a crewmember for each of the former clients and told them to watch them like a hawk. Don't let them out of your sight, and don't let them hide anything on board.

After they'd left, I then told the crew to take the boat apart. I didn't want any hidden stashes left on my boat. If I found any powder I couldn't account for, it was going over the side. It was a hell of a lot of work, we didn't find anything, and we lost some clients, but it was more than worth it to get that kind of garbage off my boat.

Sometimes, though, the surprises could be amusing. I remember one time, in the first year, the crew was sitting around, talking about what they'd done and jobs they'd worked before coming aboard the *Honor*. Dave, one of the deckhands, had been a Marine. He knew his job, was a good worker, and sure as hell didn't create any drama. I was glad to have him on the boat. But he sure amazed our first officer, Alan, when he filled the crew in on one item on his résumé: gay porn. Alan's jaw just fell to the floor, he was so shocked. Everyone cracked up, since they just had no idea. Can't judge a book by its cover. But hell, if everyone who worked in porn was as good a worker as Dave and as nice, I'd recruit Adult Video News Award nominees to work my boat.

It's certainly a unique experience living and working at sea. It's not like other jobs, where you punch in, do your work, and punch out. For us, punching in might take a few days, or a few months. When you finally do have some downtime, it's going to be shared with the same people you spend all day working with. When you go to sleep, chances are good that your coworkers are your roommates as well. It can make things filled with more tension and stress, but can also create a strong bond, like family. Who else spends all day together and then also lives together? Sometimes, you get along well with your brothers and sisters, and sometimes you don't. But you make the best of it because that's all you can do.

Working on a TV show has been a learning experience, but at the same time, it hasn't changed who I am or what I do. First and foremost, I'm still a captain, a sailor. Whether there are cameras there or not, I do my job, try to keep the clients safe, try to keep my crew safe, and try to keep the boat in good shape. It's like I tell everyone who works for me: don't embarrass yourself or the boat, and things will work out fine.

I've got a lot more people who know who I am now, but I don't think working in TV has changed me. If you thought I was a decent guy before, I'm still a decent guy. If you thought I was an asshole before, then that's equally unchanged. It's all I know how to be.

For better or worse, I'm thankful for that, because I'm incredibly appreciative for the life I've led. I wasn't born with a clear path marked out for me way in advance. I worked as a welder because the pay was good, and it let me do something that few people had the skills or the backbone even to attempt. When prospects in manufacturing started drying up, I decided to own a bar and restaurant, because it seemed exciting and because I loved the idea of being my own boss. Sometimes those days were good, sometimes those days were hard. But it's because of becoming a restaurant owner that I came to Turks and Caicos, and that's what got me my start working on the high seas.

Once I got a taste of that, I knew I'd finally found my calling. It had the excitement of working the high steel, the beauty of living in a place of infinite horizons, and eventually it had the freedom of being the boss. Every day is different. Every minute provides new problems to solve, new dangers to navigate, new paths to chart. It's not a life or a career that everyone would want. If it were, then it wouldn't be for me. It takes a lot of hard work and character, and you always stand up for what you believe to be right. I had a lot of luck, some good, some bad, but it's exactly the life I want to live. I've faced sharks and barracudas, corrupt cops in third-world countries, and some very dedicated Coast

Guardsmen who always eventually had my back. I've run into devastating storms and survived. I've been on the receiving end of my share of punches and gave as good if not better than I got in return. At the end of the day, I'm the captain of my boat and my life, and I'm exactly where I want to be.

Acknowledgments

I'd like to thank my sister Victoria for helping me find a title for this book. This book would not have been possible without Frances Berwick, who championed *Below Deck* and was instrumental in providing encouragement to start writing down some of my stories. I'd like to thank Shari Levine, Doug and Rebecca Henning, Mark Cronin, and Courtland Cox, whose brilliance, energy, and drive helped get our show off the ground and where it is today. Finally, I'd like to thank my buddy Raj, without whose support and advice I wouldn't be here.